For Mom and Dad

Sticksville   Marc Breslin

Zolo Press

Peter Paul Biggums

Peter Paul Biggums ran for mayor of Sticksville in 1983, 1987, and again in 1995. All attempts were unsuccessful. Each time his slogan was "If You Fuck Up Once, Don't Do It Again."

On the 1983 campaign, this tagline drew widespread condemnation from the people of Sticksville. One resident, Susan Shreigley, was quoted in the local newspaper, *The Times of Sticksville*, as saying, "I can't believe a potential public servant would utter profanity like that, let alone make it his motto. It's disgusting for me." Jane Rutland, another resident, agreed: "What an idiot."

Biggums did have his supporters, though. Charles Bradley, the local high school Phys. Ed. teacher remarked,

To anybody who doesn't agree with the way Pete talks or how he chooses to represent himself, let me ask you this, let me ask you this. If you're a hungry mouse and you see a piece of cheese on the floor, you're going to eat it. You're going to eat it. But let's say that piece of cheese is actually inside of a trap, and when you go to get it, the silvery-bar-thing nearly chops your head off. Are you going to go to the next piece of cheese right next to the previous one and try to get it? No. Because you F'd up the first time, nearly had your mouse head swiped off your little hairy mouse body and you don't want to die. Get it? Jesus, people, it's not Phys. Ed. or rocket science.

(Note to reader: Charles Bradley and Peter Paul Biggums both attended Sticksville High where they played basketball and were known to cheat on their math, science, and social studies tests together. Further note to reader: Your writer also attended Sticksville High with Charles Bradley and Peter Paul Biggums, and saw them cheat on multiple occasions.)

Four years later, in 1987, Peter Paul Biggums is back on the ballot with the same motto as his previously unsuccessful 1983 run: "If You Fuck Up Once, Don't Do It Again." At the 1987 Sticksville Mayoral Debate, moderator

Jessica Silverdreme inquired, "Mr. Biggums, after all of the controversy over your slogan for the 1983 Sticksville mayoral campaign, and your subsequent loss to incumbent Gerald Leftway, why have you chosen to use the same slogan?" Peter Paul Biggums responded:

Mrs. Silverdreme, to the people of Sticksville, and my opponents, I stand before you tonight as not only your neighbor and your local Credit Union of Sticksville employee, but as someone who has fucked up and will probably fuck up again. I can't even begin to tell you how many times I've fucked up or even caused others to fuck up. I got Jacky Boy arrested on breaking and entering charges in '79 for dropping him off at a stranger's house when he was hammered and telling him it was his house! I mean I'm actually just remembering, right now, here on stage, that when Tony and I were real little I convinced him that if he put weights on his balls his dick would get bigger. That makes no sense! To be totally honest, I'm amazed I haven't

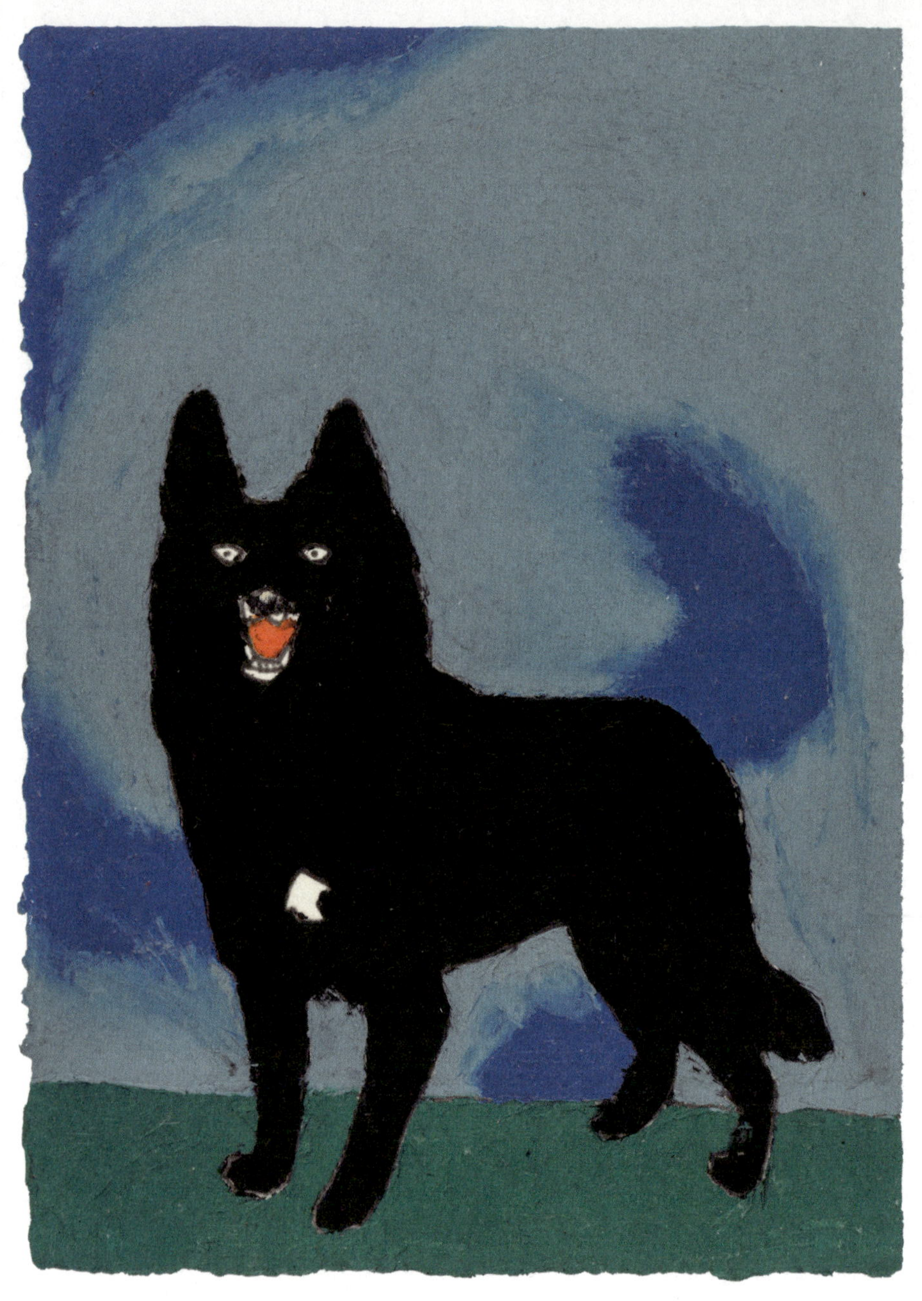

(fig. 1)

spent more than that one week in jail, back in '81 for not paying for a ski pass in New Jersey. New Jersey! And they locked me up with an alleged killer and an admitted pedophile. I mean can you imagine that! Now that's—

Jessica Silverdreme interrupted and let him know his time was up for that question, and asked him to please refrain from using obscenities or discussing private parts for the rest of the debate.

In 1987 Peter Paul Biggums finished seventh out of ten candidates for the Mayor of Sticksville. Gerald Leftway was re-elected. Peter Paul Biggums did beat out two convicted felons—turns out they were not actually allowed on the ballot—and a six-year-old Belgian Shepherd (fig. 1) whose owner (the Schmidts) took advantage of a loophole in Sticksville's Founding Members Constitution in hopes of drumming up a social media following for their dog—the Schmidts had fallen on hard times and were having trouble paying for Buddy's weekly delivery of lamb, rabbit, and whole grain rice

(Buddy being the Belgian Shepherd, that is).

Fast forward a boring eight years where nothing really happened in Sticksville—except for the closing of Sticksville Rubber Plant after a poisonous substance was found to have been leaking into the local water supply for the last seventy-five years—and Peter Paul Biggums is back on the ballot.

November 16, 1995, Sticksville High gymnasium. Peter Paul Biggums stands up from one of those too-small chairs that tall athletes have to sit on and walks to the podium. He's wearing a wrinkled, baggy black suit with a bright green shirt and gold tie with—if you were in the front row, you could see—little dolphins smoking cigarettes on it (fig. 2), white Sketcher weird arc walking shoes (fig. 3), and he's got gel in his hair that makes it look sharp in a dangerous way. Here are his opening remarks, taken verbatim from a VHS recording found in the archives at Sticksville Town Hall:

> To the great people of Sticksville, my fellow candidates and to all those people that aren't with us tonight, I stand before you.

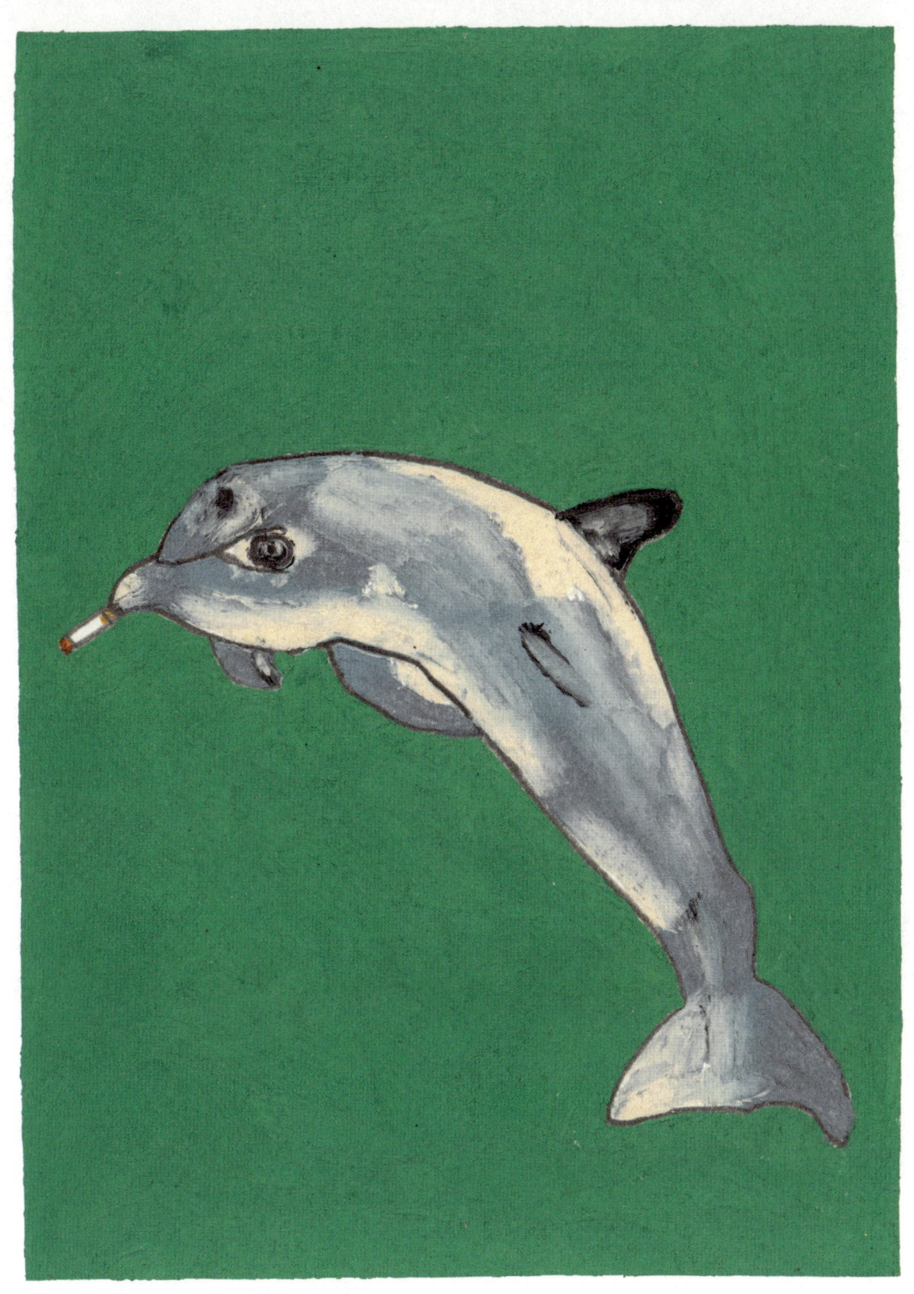

(fig. 2)

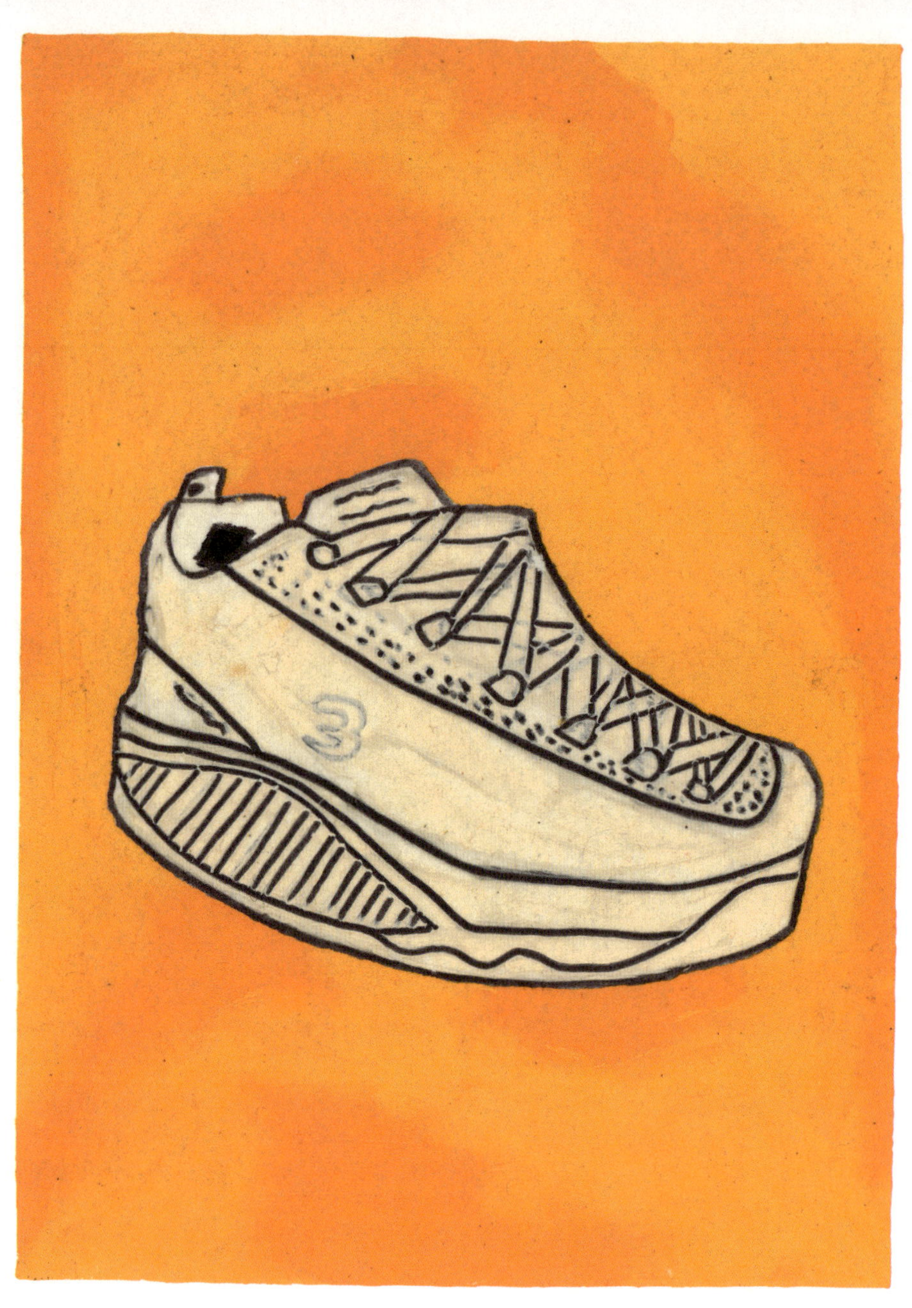

(fig. 3)

Look. Take a good, hard look. You trust me every day to not look at your PIN when you type it into the little machine-thingy, and not to steal money from your bank accounts. You trust me to file the right paperwork for your mortgages and loans. When you put your debit card in that little machine-thingy and ask to take money out, have I ever kept a twenty for myself or told you that there are some *hidden fees associated with the account that need to be adjusted for at this time?* Well, did I, or do I do that? Do I do that? No. And why? Why don't I steal or tell you things that aren't true? Because I used to steal all the time and lie all the time. Even about little, stupid things. Like when strangers would drive through town and ask for directions, I'd tell them things I knew were wrong. Or back on the '87 campaign when I felt threatened by Buddy, did I poison him in the Schmidts' backyard as I could have very easily done? Did I? In '92 when Larry Kingles pulled me over and arrested me for drunk driving, did I lose my shit and protest and try to get out of it? No, I told him exactly how many beers and cocktails I'd had—hell, even how many toots I did at Boosey's. I spent five days in jail and paid almost half my yearly salary from the Credit Union for that fuck up. But that's exactly my point. I never got caught again. I never killed Buddy. Never stole a single dime from the Union, or from you. Haven't lied since that one time when I told myself I just can't lie anymore. I even took last night off from boozing cause I was so nervous about getting up here and making this speech. I stand before you—sober, yes, defeated twice before, yes—in a suit I borrowed from my friend Chuck. *If You Fuck Up Once, Don't Do It Again!*

Peter Paul Biggums came in fifth place in the 1995 Sticksville mayoral race.

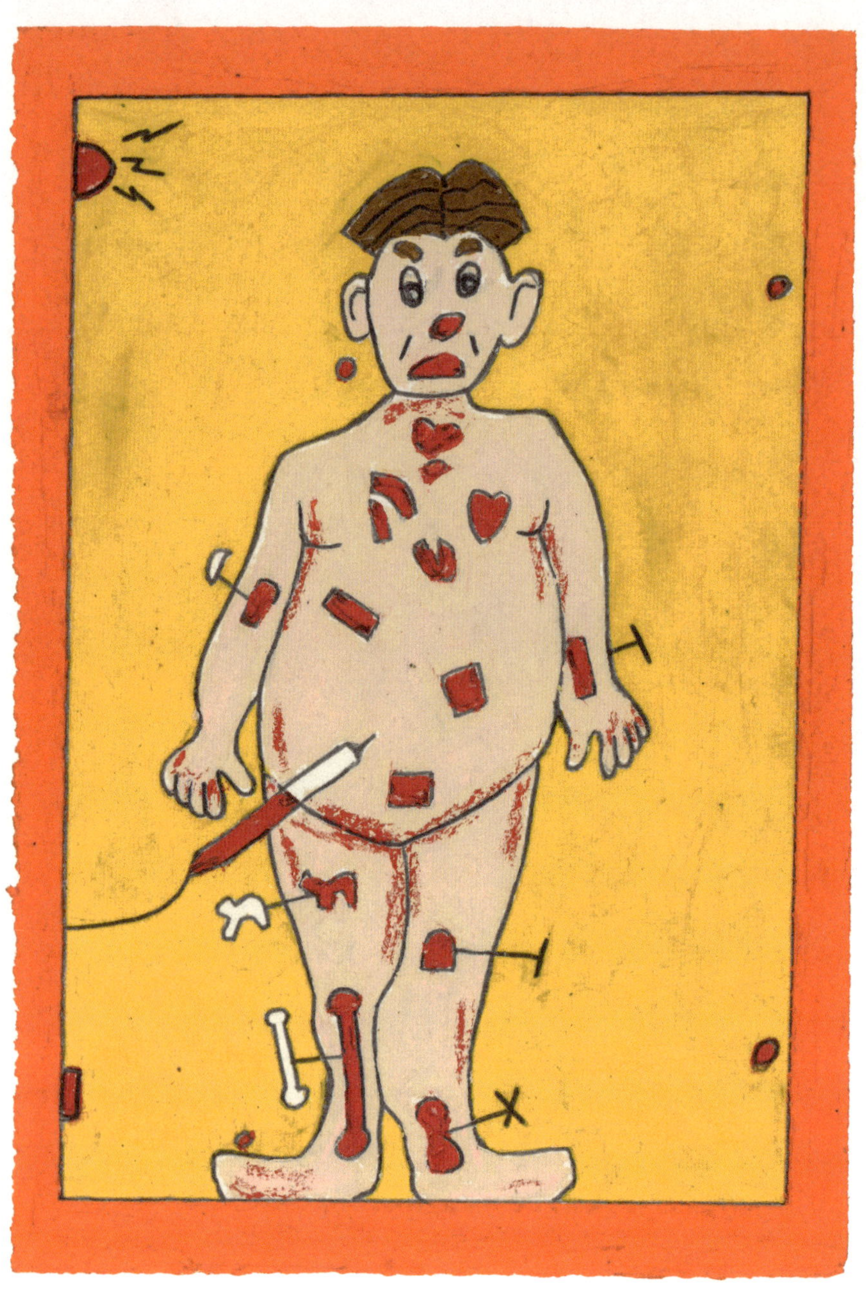

(fig. 4)

Danny Rodriguez

Danny Rodriguez was sick of playing Operation
(fig. 4) and looking for Waldo with his little
sister Tammy. Tammy is nine years younger
than Danny. Danny is fifteen. Last night, Jane
Baldwin touched Danny's dick. This marked
the first time someone had touched Danny's
dick other than him touching it in the shower,
him also touching it when he peed, and Doctor
Simpson squeezing his balls and making him
cough, which he thought strange and cruel of his
parents who arranged this meeting every year.
I guess Doctor Simpson doesn't qualify since he
didn't really touch Danny's dick. But that was it.
Doctor Simpson was the only person who'd seen
his penis, besides Mr. and Mrs. Rodriguez of
course. And now Jane. *Ahhhh, Jane.* With those
green eyes and that short, blond hair.

Danny'd been watching her since Tammy,
Mom and Dad, and him moved to Sticksville
from Los Angeles two years ago. This transition
positively sucked for Danny Rodriguez. Cursing
and rock-hard boners had recently taken over

Danny's conscious mind. His subconscious was
also dominated by foul phrases and images of
rock-hard boners. For the better part of seventh
and eighth grades, Danny thought he might
be gay because of the nonstop, conscious and
subconscious bombardment of boners. But then
there was last night.

Dad was driving everyone back from Tim
Callinan's birthday party. Best friend Steve
Schmidt was sitting up front, talking with
Dad about tectonic plate displacement and the
horrible second half loss the New York Jets
suffered to the Jacksonville Jaguars. Back right
seat was Diana Sinclair Gutierrez, looking out
the window and mouthing the lyrics to what
Danny thought was some cheesy Backstreet
Boys song. And in the middle was Jane. Dad'd
offered the two girls a ride since they were
staying at Diana's in Pleasant Greens, the next
community over from Deer Creek Terrace where
Danny lives. It happened on Mill Street Road,
right after they'd passed the Citgo station and
Go Bagel Me (fig. 5).

Danny was also looking out the window—
pretending he was skateboarding, grinding

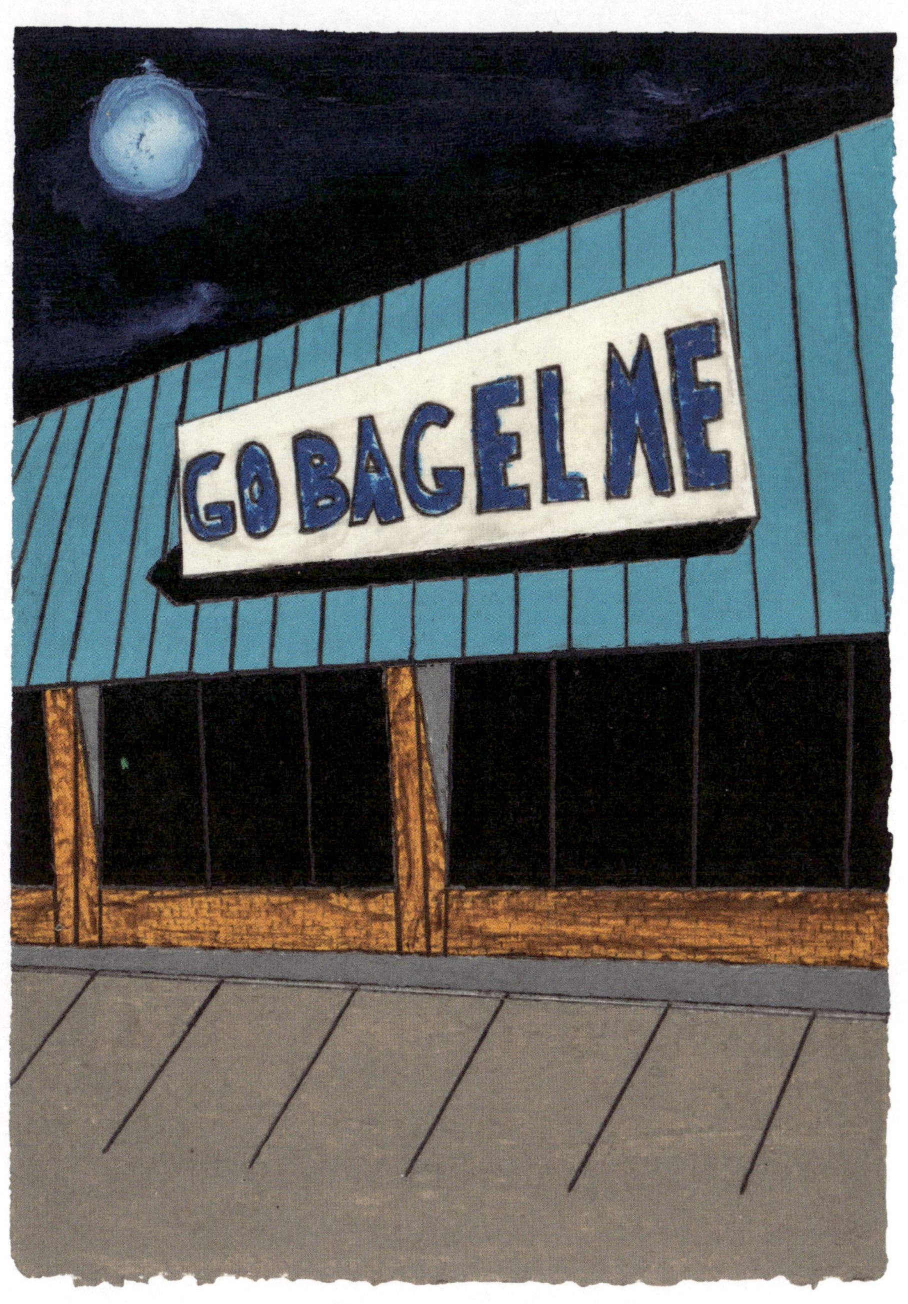

(fig. 5)

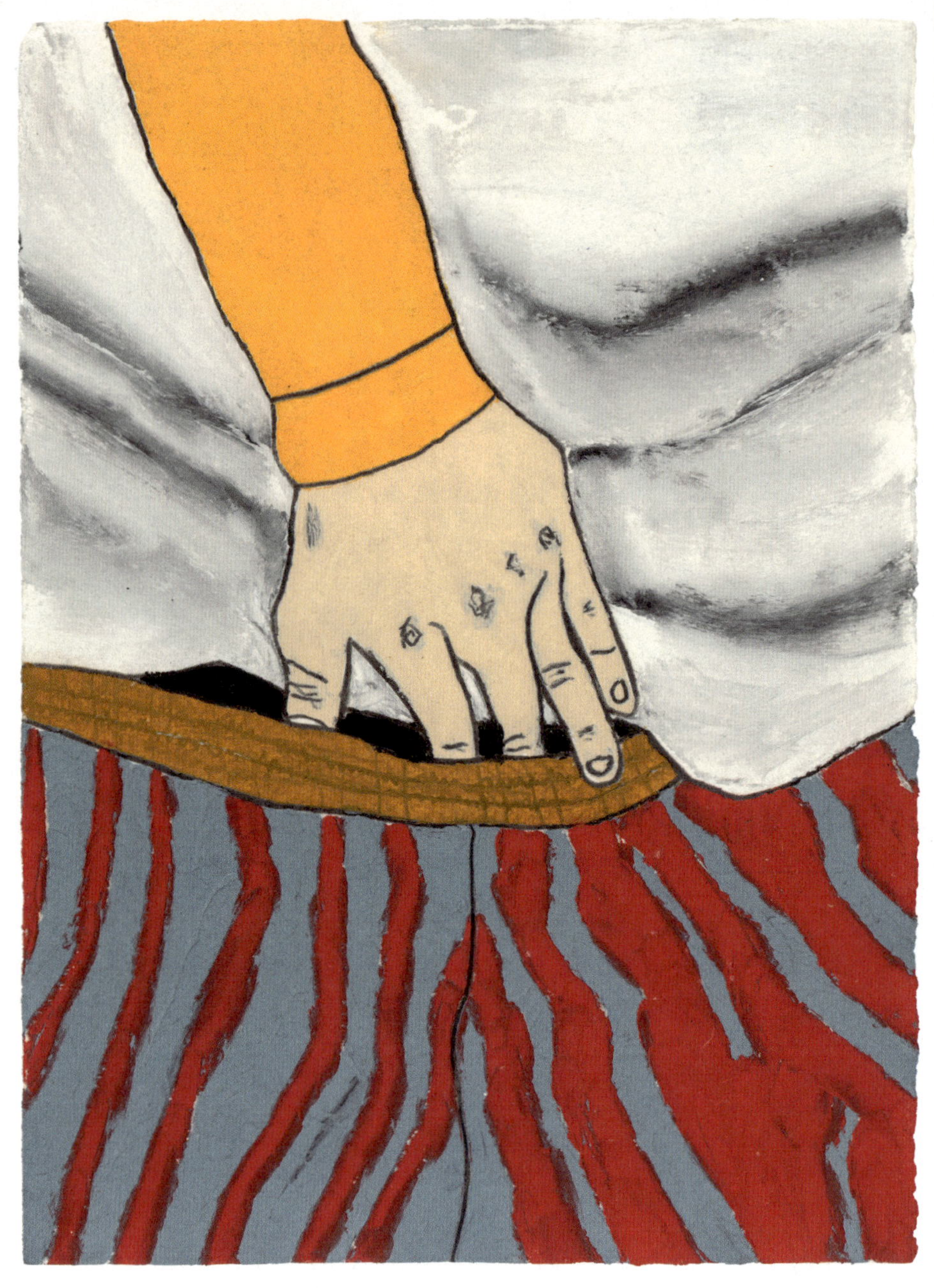

(fig. 6)

the guardrails, weaving around the stop signs and doing a heel-flip outside the Go Bagel Me parking lot—when he felt Jane's left hand first slip between his pants and his underwear (fig. 6). He kept looking out the window and then she readjusted and this time slid between his underwear and skin. Now he turned to look at her and she kept staring right ahead, pretending to pay attention to what Steve was saying about a tectonic plate shift that just happened in the Pacific Northwest and had set off a series of earthquakes and tsunamis that only affected aquatic life. Danny saw his dad look back in the rearview mirror and they caught eyes. Was Dad smiling? He *was*. Danny could tell by the way his eyes were squinting. And Danny, with Jane's left hand fishing around his crotch, smiled back.

"Danny."

"Uhh, yes Dad?"

"What do you make of that loss?"

"What? I mean, I'm sorry. What are you talking about?"

"Steven and I have been talking about the Jet's loss tonight. That horrible second-half loss. What of it?"

With Jane's hand still groping and probing, Danny rattled off phrases and stats he'd heard with his mom earlier on the radio. "I gotta be honest with you, Dad. The Jets were putting up points on offense, defense—hell—even special teams tacked some points on the board. And then there was the halftime, and what followed was one of the saddest things I've witnessed in the NFL. It's like they ran out of gas and things just started falling apart. They got sloppy. Dwayne Jones ran for 143 yards in the first half and only got two touches in the second. Bo Riddles (fig. 7) threw 12/13 for 248 yards in the first and then 3/18 for 32 yards in the second, plus an interception. I don't know, Dad. In my opinion, it was a combination of bad stamina and poor coaching that made this one of the worst second-half losses I've ever seen in my life."

This whole time, Jane had been playing with him and, without knowing it, Danny was rock-hard and Jane looked at him. Danny looked at her. What the fuck am I talking about, Danny thought. Danny, happy about his boner, realized two things during this drive. One: I am not gay. Two: or am I? What kind of man can rattle off

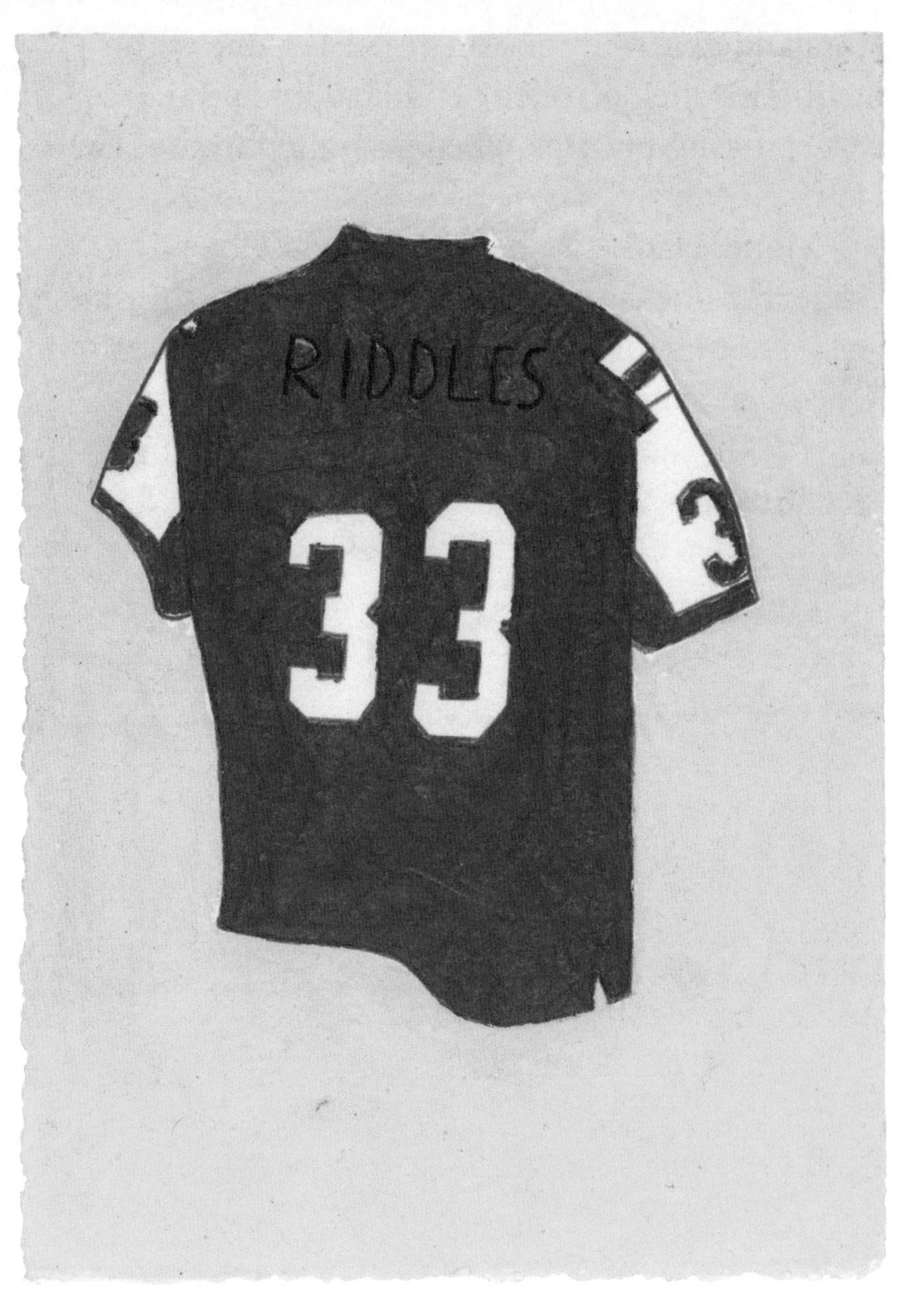

(fig. 7)

stats and give opinions on an NFL game while having his dick stroked? Did Dad know Jane was stroking my dick when he smiled in the rear view? No way.

"Jane, Diana, we have arrived at Chez Gutierrez. Please say hello to your parents for me."

"Thanks for the ride home Mr. Rodriguez! See you at school Monday, Steve and Danny!"

"Yeah, thanks Mr. Rodriguez. Bye Danny."

"Bye Jane."

All of a sudden, it was like everybody's mantelpiece was on my phone. You know what I mean? Like portraits, and baby pictures, and vacation pictures, and dog pictures. All those types of pictures you'd see on top of the fireplace, or going up the staircase, or on the desk in the office, or in the photo flap of an accordion wallet.

... *Dingy's recovering from the first phase of her double-radical-mastectomy. Please pray for her and keep this strong animal in your thoughts and hearts!!! #blessed*
... *Can't believe Little Ricky turned 6 months today! Can't believe what's happened in the past year! #blessed*
... *Samantha on Pearl. The bond between young girls and horses is something that's been in my family for ages. Starting with Nana Simone, my dear deceased mother, Mum, and now sharing this moment with Sam just has me feeling so grateful #blessed.*

"Hashtag Blessed." I mean. *So happy my hemorrhoids finally went away*. Hashtag Blessed. Can you believe it? So much gratitude.

Ever been to one of the several Cafe Gratitudes? If you were in the Space Station looking down at Los Angeles, or searching on Google Maps, you'd see them hop-skotchedly placed in a form roughly resembling—you knew it—Mercury in retrograde. This is taken verbatim from their website:

> We practice business through a term we call "Sacred Commerce," where we provide inspired service, honest and transparent communication, and express gratitude for the richness of our lives.

Hashtag Have A Blessed Day. I feel Blessed. Do you? No? Oh. Well. I must say— only because I too believe in this Sacred Commerce, and as commerce is just another term for communication, and communication, in my opinion, just a euphemism for speaking plainly, indeed in the best of times and the worst of times—that I'm terribly sorry for

your loss. Doesn't the model fall apart when
Doug Shinkles, who has been working at
Cafe Gratitude Venice Beach for the past sun-
blastingly-numb ten years while chasing a
career in acting (and computer science, and
also mostly pursuing a career doing CGI for
major motion picture companies) is so sad that
his boyfriend, Brad Turner—don't ask how I
know their names or that they moved to LA
together from Wyoming back in 2004, after
both failed gaining entrance to Texas A&M, but
luckily were both accepted to The University
of Wyoming, the institution's motto being,
"BUCKING THE SYSTEM SINCE 1886" as well
as "THE WORLD NEEDS MORE COWBOYS".
They met their second year at UW in the small
community of Laramie. And so on, you know.—
just broke up with him, that after telling his
third table of the morning (all fat, Midwestern,
rude, hillbilly, sunburnt-fucks he thought he'd
got away from at least six years ago) "Have a
Blessed Day!"—fake smile, leave check, close
hands in hashtag prayer mode—he loses his shit
and cries in the bathroom for fifteen minutes?
Which, by the way, created an awfully long line

and, in this economy, no matter how *sacred*, time still does equal money. And for the long shitter, sitter, and crier, that's money—I guess all puns intended—down the shitter.

Then my friend Sarah's band, Psychosluts from Hell, popped on the feed. Proper weird shit after the dogs, and babies, and Hashtag Blessed stuff. Like skeletoid aliens with fake boobs and really long nails doing all types of obscene things to regular old humans, both female and male, all with even bigger fake boobs, but these ones were fat, fully skinned, and apparently oiled-up by way of the sticks of butter they all were holding in each of their hands (fig. 8). Pretty full-on and somehow these posters for their shows made me like them even more. At the bottom of the image:

Psychosluts from Hell play TONIGHT
⚡⚡⚡ *FREE SHOW* ⚡⚡⚡
sorry babes 🙁 *18+ @hueyshouseofhorrors,*
748 W. Main Rd, Loz Anguhleez, Calif.
@tobleronehoes & @cindysondarag
are opening. Doors at 8.
DONT FUCKING MISS IT.

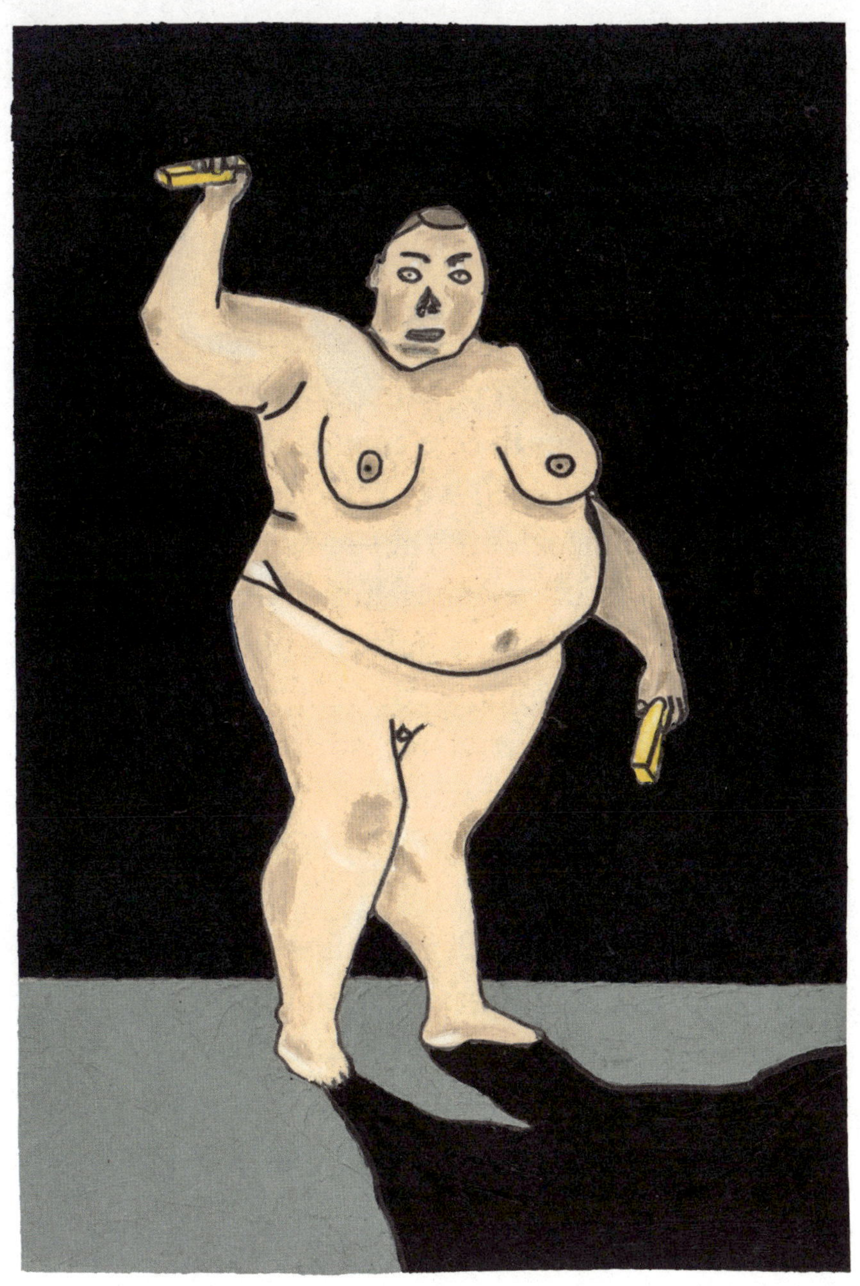

(fig. 8)

Sarah tagged me in these and they always ended in some type of threat or warning—"DONT FUCKING MISS IT." Or at least because I knew Sarah so well, that's how I interpreted them. The period also helped. No time or mood for exclamation points.

I rarely missed a show. I saw them way back when there were three people in attendance standing underneath one carport while the Psychosluts from Hell were five feet away from us underneath another carport at our friend Stephanie's parents' house in Altadena. Now Sarah was on tour half the year and they had become a movement, or a part of other ones that found their lyrics, sound, and stage presence in tune with whatever their core values were—kind of like Cafe Gratitude, but different.

The last time the Psychosluts were in LA I had a one-night-stand with the oddest looking girl I've ever seen, let alone slept with. She looked more like something I remember reading about in one of J.R.R. Tolkien's books when I was a kid—before I saw the movies and they wrecked my visuals of the characters and landscapes. Okay, not like one of the dwarves or a lady hobbit, not the scary queen, not Gollum, but a combination of all of them in a flat, 2D type of way. The morning after, we ate pizza with root beers and took a long walk around the reservoir, where we saw lots of Hashtag Blessed moments in the dog park and couples with strollers, etc., chatting away and me feeling oddly loose and natural—I guess I was feeling a little Hashtag Blessed, too—before I had to catch a plane back home to Sticksville. And for some reason—it only hit me when I was stuck in a middle seat between two standins for a future Psychosluts from Hell poster—I realized I didn't get her number and was her name Josephine or Mary? To be honest, I just thought I'd run into her again, like how we'd met.

Toblerone Hoes were already on stage when I arrived at Huey's House of Horrors, 8:30 P.M. There were probably forty or fifty people there, and the place was dead quiet. But the crowd was transfixed. Apparently this is a band that doesn't play music. The six band members were wearing costumes that made them look like huge packages of Toblerone, with the mountains and colors, perforation at the top, everything perfect and very well made. They had their stage names printed on the package like you can sometimes find in Italy, or on Coke cans in gas stations—more of the Hashtag Blessed, Cafe Gratitude type of "Sacred Commerce" in my opinion—and apparently they were in the middle of a play where Joy was fucking Pain hard in the corner—like had Pain bent, nearly doubled, over—Sweet and Sour were splayed in front of the crowd playing with themselves, and Panic and Chill were boxing in the other corner, stage left, with real boxing gloves on, pummeling one another. I was staring at this shit when someone tapped me on the shoulder and scared the hell out of me.

"Jesus, Pete. Relax."

"You scared the hell out of me, Sarah. What the fuck is this?"

"What? This? *Those* are the Toblerone Hoes. I found them in Louisiana when I was playing a show there. Some underground, gay party-thing where—"

Somebody hushed us and I almost cringed. I've been in this scenario before with Sarah, like at a movie, or play, even a funeral, where she's talking at her normal level, which for everybody else is super loud, and they ask her to be respectful, or to please be quiet, or *shhhhhhhush* her and this happens, which is what happened just now. "Shut the fuck up, turn around, and keep watching the chocolate fuck," she answered. I could never talk to anyone like that. Makes me shakey. "Anyway, I fell in love with these chocolate fuckers and they've been on tour with me all year."

The Toblerone Hoes stopped *playing* and I could tell not because I saw Panic actually KO Chill or every other piece of chocolate reach climax, but because the place was actually silent.

"Nice buzz, huh?" Sarah said. And that was it. They had this droned-out buzz playing the whole time which only registered as sound now that it had stopped. And for those who had never seen The Toblerone Hoes before, this was more than just cool; it was transcendental. I told Sarah I was going outside for a smoke. Had to get some fresh air. Makes no sense, but smoking in the fresh air is nicer. Also was hoping to see Josephine or Mary.

I went back in and Cindy's On Da Rag was setting up her synth and guitar (fig. 9). At the bar I ordered another mezcal margarita (fig. 10)—the first one already talking to me—and checked the scene again. Audience had doubled, like up to maybe eighty or a hundred, I mean I have no idea, but it was full. But somehow all of the guys had disappeared. Only women. Weird.

I'd never heard of Cindy before, didn't know what her music was like, but it struck me, I was on a Mission Impossible. I wasn't sure if her name was Josephine or Mary, or either of those—could be Ginger—and it was like when my pitbull Pokey ran away and I looked all over the Internet for lost pitbulls at all of the shelters and I was no longer able to recall what my dog looked like. My dear dog. I felt terrible when that happened and this somehow was the same, except I was at a severe disadvantage already; I'd slept with Pokey every night not including when I was traveling for seven years. I only slept with Josephine, Mary, or Ginger one night, and the next morning, once pretty locked in, was fading. And the crowd of only women made it seem like finding an old friend after landing on the far side of moon.

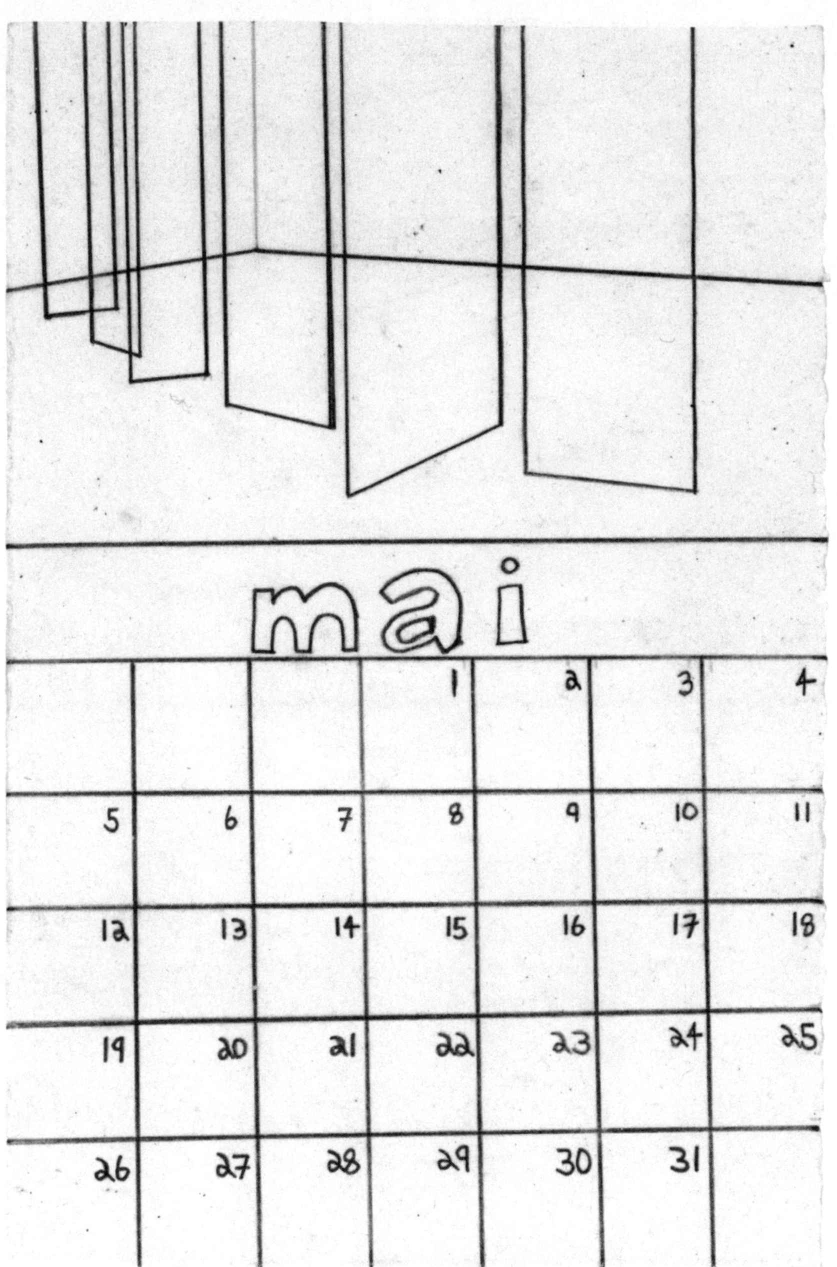

(fig. 9)

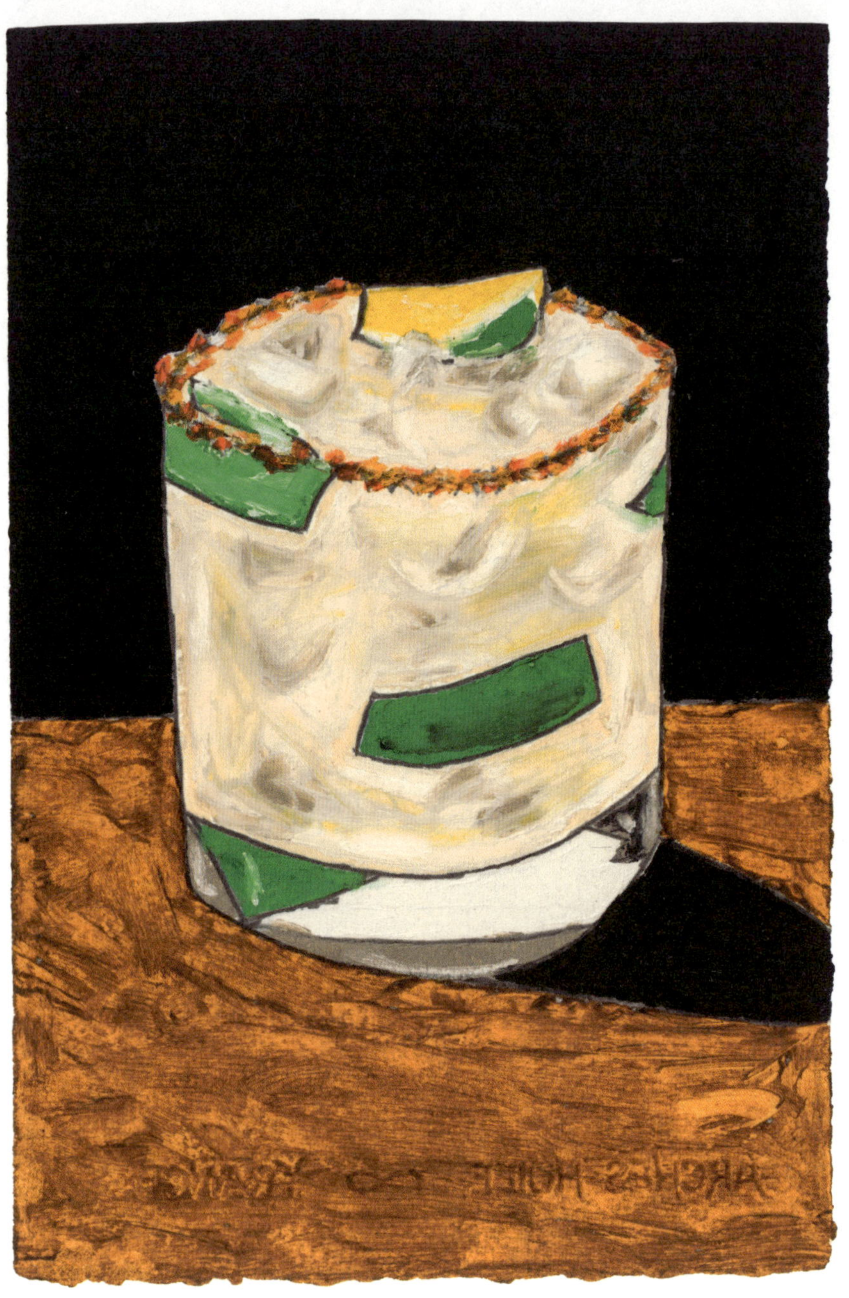

(fig. 10)

Like, "Hey You! Watcha doin here?!?!?" Big Hug. "Shall we catch up over delicious Kona Brewery Big Wave beer I have here on tap in my moon lander?" Not happening. And Cindy sucked. Like a bad guitar player with whiny lyrics and super pop synth stuff. I must say she had her admirers. Everybody in the crowd knew all the words to her songs; some people were crying.

I slithered through the audience and the feeling was intense. A few women gave me nasty looks and one nudged me out of the way because, for a second, I'd blocked her view. I finally found Sarah at the farthest part of the horseshoe bar. She started before I could ask.

"I know, man. Don't ask why I like her. I won't make you tell me why you don't. But her name really is Cindy. She's like twenty-six and she does one show a month when she's literally on the rag. All those chicks, they are too. It's like this wave of emotion and they all got on the same cycle. Pretty powerful shit, man. Hey, you want this? I'm going on soon and don't wanna be hammered."

I took her drink and wondered: *twenty-six*? Thought she was forty-something. Another mezcal margarita. My buddy, Sarah. She hadn't taken a sip. Salt all intact. She knew I'd be like a kid at a music festival who'd just lost his friends, tripping hard on mushrooms, or acid, or Molly, or a combo of those, bugging out. Sarah knew I was looking for her and was more than ready for my arrival. I didn't have to say or do anything. Just take her drink and her seat at the bar, from which I'd be able to watch her and the other Psychosluts play.

11 P.M. on the dot. Place is officially jammed. Crowd mixed, whatever that means. But things are electric. The Psychosluts from Hell are old-school punk rock. Bass, guitar, and drums with a synth. Sarah plays guitar and synth, her girlfriend Diana is on bass, and Diana's younger sister Jessica is on drums. They're heavily influenced by Bad Brains— Sarah saw them play a lot with her older brother while growing up in D.C.—and by Bill Callahan. So like Bad Brains, but instead of switching between reggae and punk rock, the Psychosluts switched between punk rock and these slow, elegiac melodies with lyrics that showed Sarah's vulnerability.

This is Sarah. Hardcore, no bullshit, but sweet and thoughtful. Caring, but doesn't give a fuck. I once asked her why she named her band Psychosluts. She said, "We are women on earth. Psychosluts from Hell is just to let the dudes in."

After a heavy duty, break-the-stage-and-fuck-shit-up rocker jam—everyone wet with sweat—there was a momentary silence. Real silence, no buzz, maybe collective breathing, and Sarah says, "I wanna dedicate this one to my buddy Pete, sitting in the way back of the bar." A spotlight hidden the whole show comes on and blasts me. I can't see fucking anything and it kinda hurt, so I covered my eyes. "Hey Pete. This one's for you." I looked up and through a severe, sun-like haze could begin to make out body parts and then could focus even better. The whole place looking at me. Sarah: "Everybody on three, FUCK YOU PETE! 1–2–3!"

A massive jet engine roar: "FUCK YOU PETE!"

Then shit went nuts and everybody was slamming into one another. Those were the only lyrics to the song, "Fuck You Pete!" It was a short one, kinda like the refrain from

The Descendents and The Queers' "This Place Sucks." They say "this place sucks" three times fast and then it's over.

And then the show actually was over. Despite feeling incredibly happy that Sarah singled me out and I got to have a couple hundred people collectively tell me to fuck off, I realized that though there was no chance of seeing Mary, Ginger, or Josephine at that concert, she for sure would have seen me because of the whole spotlight thing. I was walking home, ears and head buzzing, when I saw the text that had been sitting in my pocket since 9:37 P.M., right when Cindy and her followers were wailing and sobbing together.

> *Hey Pete*
> *I got your number from Sarah*
> *Told her I couldn't make it cause I have an early job*
> *Plus I really don't like Cindy and her weirdo gang of menstruating women* 😳
> *You have my number now* 😘
> *Dylan*

Dylan! Jesus! How could I forget that? And Sarah. Of course they're friends. Sarah did that whole "Fuck You Pete" thing cause she knew I came basically to find Dylan—thank God not Josephine, thank Jesus not Mary or Ginger, and thank her parents for giving her a boy's name. And she did the whole spotlight thing to put me in check. What a friend. What a woman. What a planet.

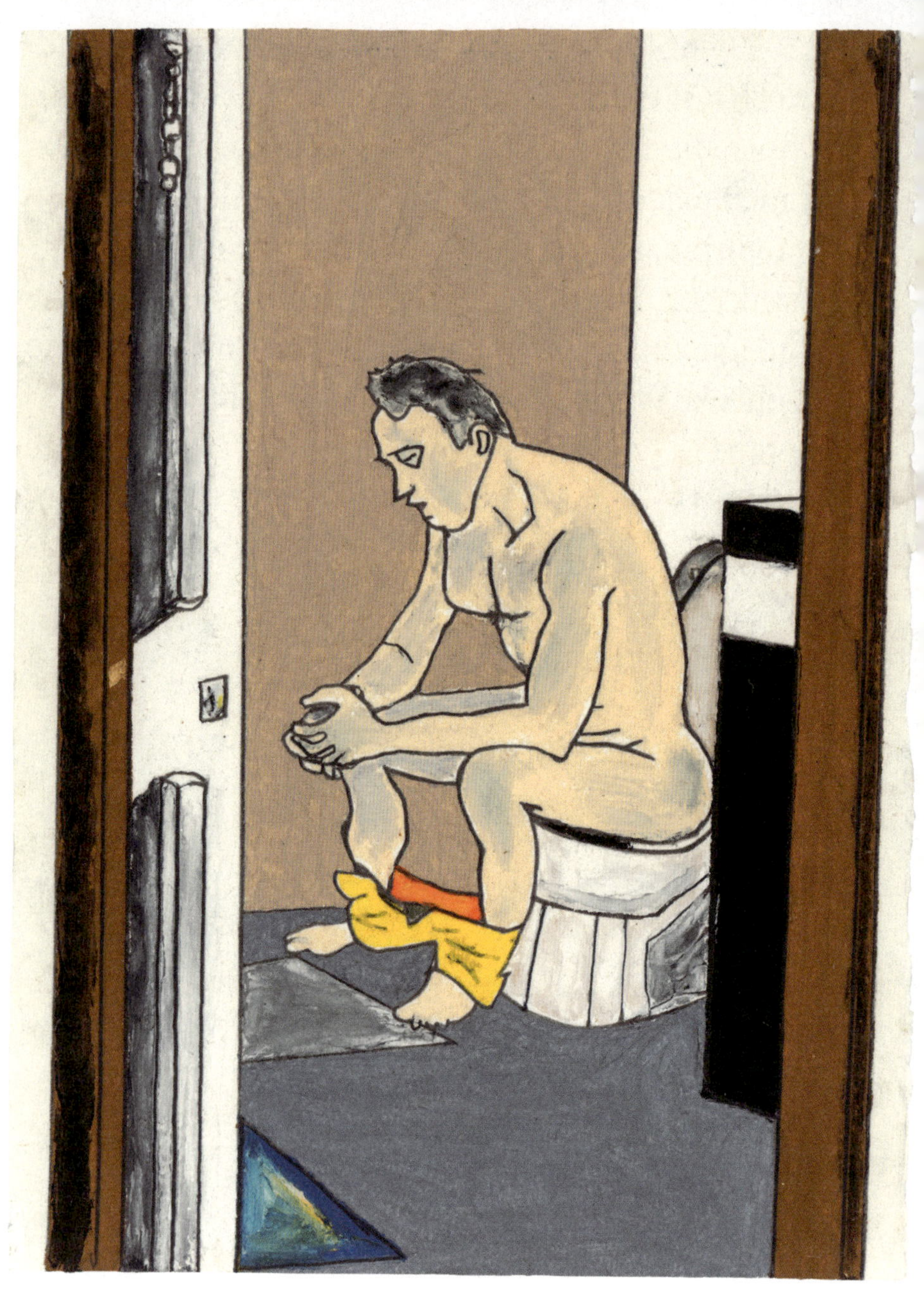

(fig. 11)

Buttons

Huey came downstairs. I was awake—on the toilet (fig. 11), actually, thinking about ancient things—when he walked into the bathroom.

"Quindee, can I make a confession?"

"Yeah Huey, go for it. Good morning."

"Yeah, good morning to you too. That's kinda what I'm talkin about. I haven't got one hard-on since we've been here. Isn't that weird? Like nothin'. No morning wood, no slight roll-overs, no nothin. Watched a li'l porn last night and it was kinda like watchin' a drama or romantic comedy. I got into their characters like I was Gene Siskel, and My Little Buddy was my happy, big-eyed friend Roger Ebert, criticizing the *film* the whole time. I mean, look. It's like a button on a jacket, or a light switch (fig. 12). It weighs a gram, I bet."

And he was right. It did look like a button (fig. 13). All small head and basically no shaft. "Me too man. I was just thinking about that now. And I tried jerking off, too. Nada. Like, *is something wrong?* Nada."

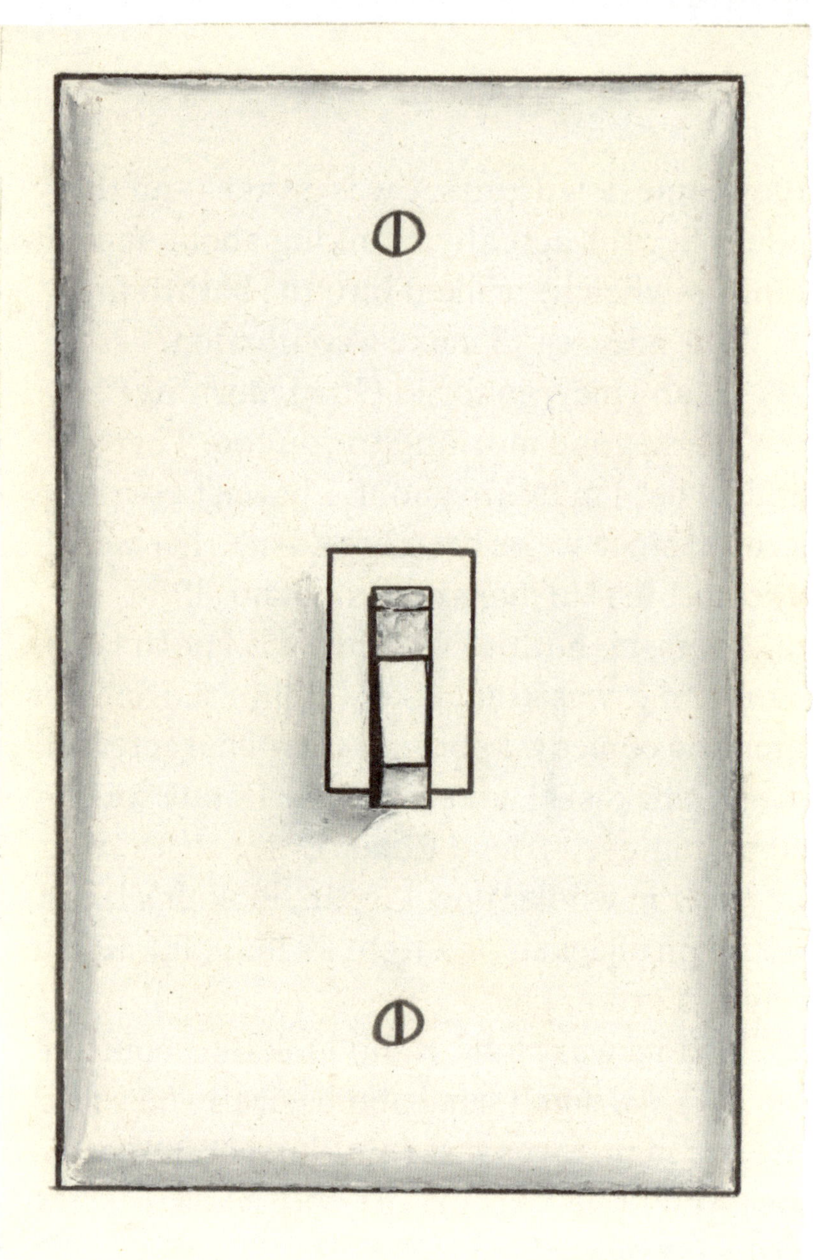

(fig. 12)

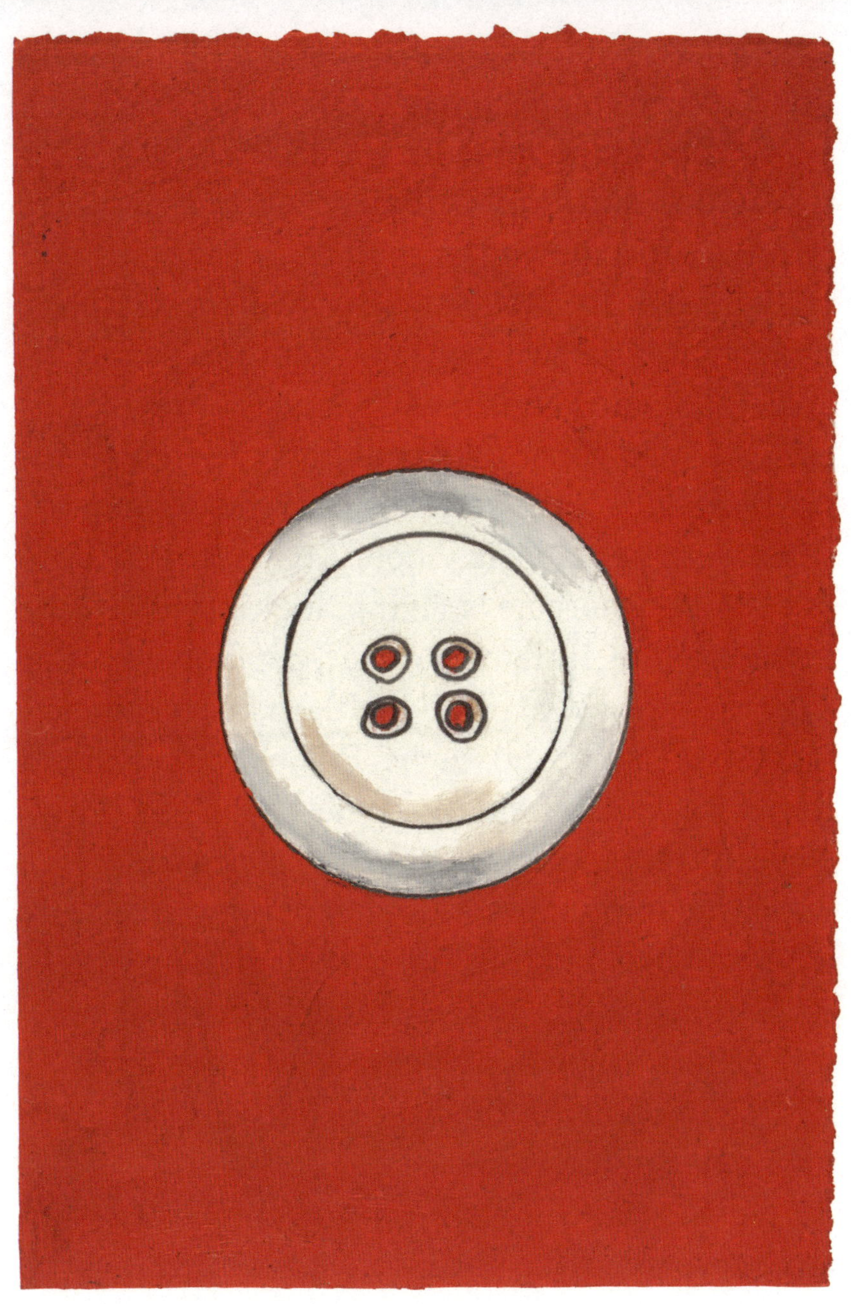

(fig. 13)

"Okay. Well, that makes me feel better. Why don't you wrap up and we'll go out for breakfast."

"Okay. Good morning, Huey."

"Good morning, Quindee."

We drove down the road to the town of Delicias. Really. Delicias is basically a stretch of asphalt with two mini-markets across the street from one another. The one we prefer is called Super Mario. Their old plastic sign on the post outside on the street is from the Nintendo series—to be specific, Super Mario Bros. 3 (fig. 14)—where he is flying, looking part little-red-suit-Italian-plumber, part leopard, and part fox—he always looked like a beaver to me; maybe it was the mustache. Some artifact that'd found its way to a small village that this family cleverly adopted as the name of their store. Super meaning market. Mario being the red guy who also had a big-eyed friend who hung out with him, although rarely now thinking about it. The most they hang out is in Mario Kart—Nintendo 64 being the best variety for that particular game.

Inside was Silby, who would cook us eggs and serve us coffee until we couldn't drink

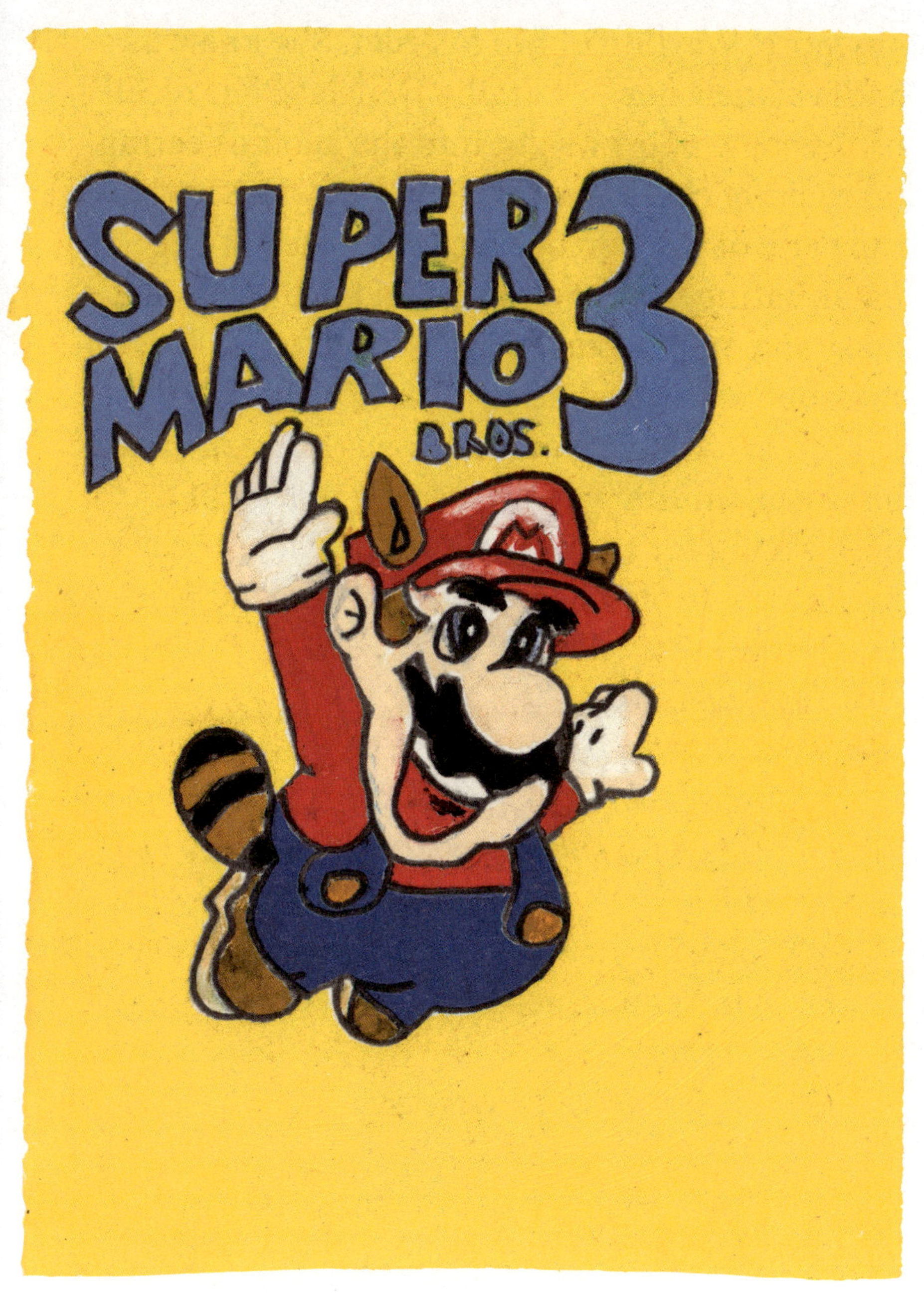

(fig. 14)

anymore. We didn't have to order. She knew us
and we knew her—"Familia Delicias," she'd call
us. At some point we got into the habit of eating
on rocking chairs outside Super Mario 3 with
the plate of eggs on our lap, the coffee in one
hand, eating with the other hand. No utensils.
Dust and animal smells. Rocking after Selby
took our plates and offered us more coffee.

I don't know what Huey was thinking about,
but I was thinking about writing to a girl I'd
been seeing for the past month and sending her a
random multiple-choice question text message:

Hey Dylan
How are you? I know this is weird but would
you mind letting me know what you think?
Then I'll tell you what I think. Have you
been:
A) *súper horny since I left*—my phone was
on Spanish settings
B) *normal*
C) *no sex drive whatsoever*

I sent it and found myself staring at the two
check marks—well, first one, then a slow two

grey check marks—waiting for them to turn blue. WhatsApp. I actually caught myself staring at the two grey check marks. Like zoomed in on them. That was when I realized, obviously, that she must know my answer was a fucking big old capital *C*.

I recently read somewhere about "ghosting" which I think is when someone starts typing and a little grey box appears with three circles suggesting something as in "DOT DOT DOT," and then nothing. I didn't really read the article. Just looked at pictures. I'd thought that ghosting was when dudes took the condom off without informing or gaining consent, but then researched and found that is called "stealthing." Either way, I immediately felt transparent. Quickly: two blue check marks. [typing]

Hey Pete—my real name
Actually a little sick. Everybody is sick.
hahahahaha
Funny question! 😂
Why do you ask?
Go swimming for me.
How are things going down there?

Big old *phew*! She is cool. I don't mess around on the messaging and emails and stuff. The first person I worked for was like this and I admired her for it. No games. No abusing a system that was meant to speed things up, only to slow them down. Like, what's your fax number? Just sit by and wait for a little. A measured, short response. Effective.

Sorry to hear that.
I did for you last night. Did you feel it?

All of a sudden, the clearing in the forest. The light from the lighthouse. The ocean revealing itself like my favorite Donald Judd work located at DIA: Beacon, not too far from Sticksville. What the viewer thinks is just a solid piece of wood, like a two-inch thick piece of plywood board acting as a vertical barrier between you and some empty space behind it, as one approaches this barrier, reveals a slight slope downhill receding from the viewer in depth and distance as you get closer to what once felt like a fence. What was previously empty space is now volumetric form. A strange encounter, no matter how many times I see it. My idea of effortlessness. This exchange with Dylan felt like that artwork. Turning some weird sexual thing—aka a fence or barrier—into literally that receding in depth and distance ocean. The sea. Quick two blue check marks. [typing]

> *Ouhh yes!*
> *That was it, touched myself while thinking*
> *of your hands coming in me.*
> *It was good!*
> *Yesterday night.*

Huey and I finished our breakfast at Super Mario Bros. 3. We got in the truck and drove in loudness to the sounds of the truck's suspension breaking over holes in the ground.

Catch of the Day

I woke up to the My Little Baby toy crying. So, we got this toy from my wife, Phyllis, her mom, Carroll. You fill the back of the doll's head up with water through a small canal—always wondered what's beyond the canal—and the doll actually makes tears when it cries.

So that thing woke me up at quarter to six and then I woke the entire family up at six when I got out of bed to check the kids' room. Samantha actually woke up because I picked up her doll to kind of, like, even it out so it would stop crying, and little fake tears dropped on Sammy's face. She woke up and made this shocked, bug-eye look like she's seeing something horrible she can't keep her eyes off of for the first time. This only lasted for probably two seconds but her mouth was doing this upside-down morphing thing at the same time, which I could feel made my face do the same weird morphing thing too. Then she shrieked and everybody was up.

To be totally honest, I kind of was already up because I had to dump. Which is kind of

a nice but awful feeling at the same time—
meaning waking up because you have to dump.
It's tough to go back to bed after you've already
wiped your butt.

So it's like half-past six all of a sudden (!) and
I watched some things on the bowl like boating
accidents, people base jumping, these kids with
face tattoos, and weird, scary-looking diamond
necklaces, and motocross in the Swiss Alps on
my phone, and then I went downstairs to start
some bacon. Dingy had to go for a pee, so when
the bacon was going I took a walk with him.
Dingy really loves that first walk of the day. He
pees like eight times wherever he wants to and
usually takes at least one big poop (fig. 15). I
started to get the scented bags cause I realized I
was gagging when Dingy was doing his business.
Plus, I like to sneak in a few A.M. batty rips and
the bags help mask the weed hands.

Actually, Phyllis mentioned it to me one
morning: "I saw you gagging from the window
picking up Dingy's shit." I told her I had no
idea—thank God she didn't see me taking batty
hits!—and that it must have been kind of funny
looking. Dingy looking happy, looking at me, you

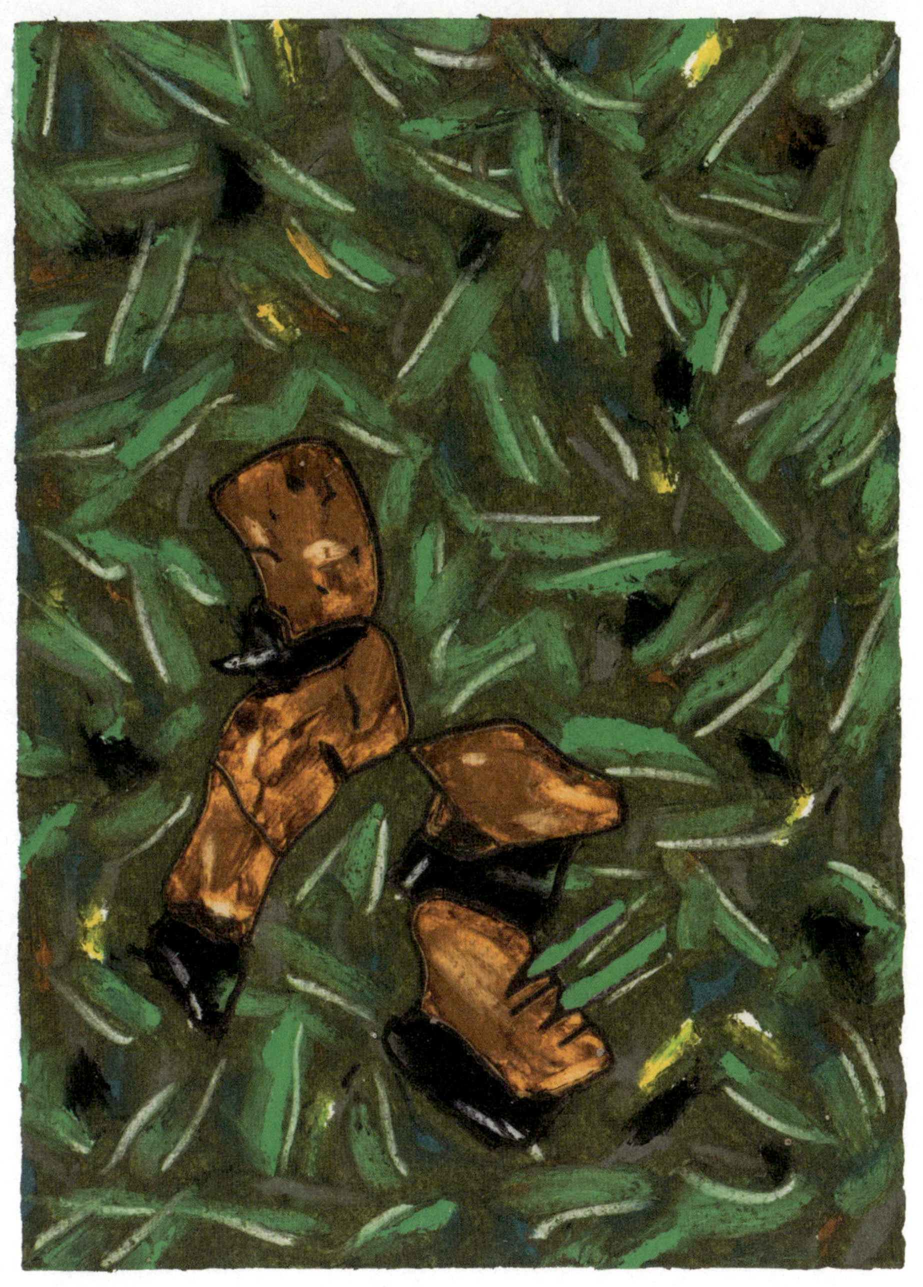

(fig. 15)

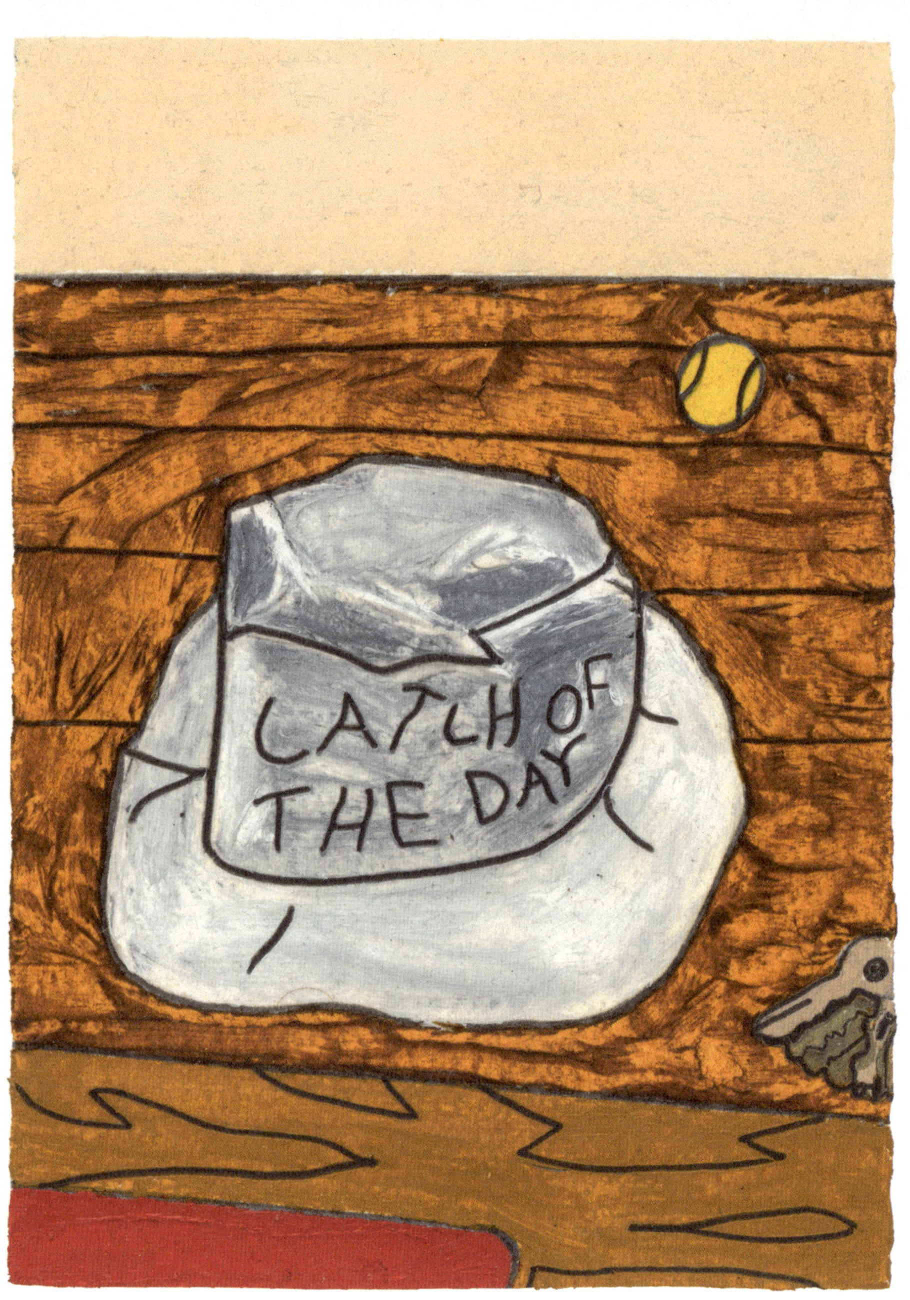

(fig. 16)

looking at us, me picking up his poop, gagging. What a scene! She said it was pretty gross and that I shouldn't leave bacon cooking in the house unattended again when I'm taking Dingy for his morning shit. I told her that made sense.

It looked like Phyllis got Sam and Viper up while Dingy was taking this weird, second, small poop where I had to pull a blade of grass out of his butt with one of the scented bags. The family looked so cute! All of them! Everybody really tired-looking with their hair all messed up, looking like they could use a nice long snooze! I cracked the eggs at 7:22 A.M. and the kids were seated and finished, looking more animated by the minute and ready for a quick rinse in the shower with their mommy. Then Daddy's taking you off to school—7:42 A.M.!

Phyllis dressed Sam in this cool ballet-dancer-fluorescent-green number with blue ballet slippers and a blue bow in her hair, and had Viper wearing purple and green '93 Jordans with vintage OshKosh B'gosh purple overalls and a little fisherman's hat that had "Catch Of The Day" written on it (fig. 16).

Eight o'clock on the dot! "Viper, Sammy, put

your seatbelts on and check your parachutes."
In the rearview mirror Viper got really serious-
looking, clicked his belt, and pretended to check
his chute, his altimeter, and put his imaginary
goggles on. Samantha looked at me in the
rearview and put her seatbelt on. On the drive
we listened to 4 Non Blondes—"Well I'm up in
the morning and I step outside and I take a deep
breath and I get real high..."—which made me
think of Dingy's poop, then two Petty songs in
a row, which made me think of my carpenter
friend, Jim, then Blind Melon's "No Rain," which
made me think of Jersey Shore summertime
boardwalk pizza and my first blowjob in a
stranger's outdoor shower, and then Sam asked
to listen to the local classical station, 92.7, in
quiet for the last ten minutes.

I was really belting out "No Rain" when I
caught Sam looking at me again in the rearview.
Was she thinking, *How is Daddy always so happy
and cheerful in the morning? How does he know
every song on the radio?* When I turned down the
radio and asked her if she was feeling okay, she
asked for the classical. Viper protested because
he loves when I sing really loud in the mornings.

He gets very excited and kind of headbangs.

So for the last ten minutes of the ride we were all very quiet. Viper fell asleep for a little and Sam looked out the window. I caught myself driving forty-five in a fifty-five, thinking about that blade of grass coming out of Dingy's butt. Next thing you know, we were entering the gate of Daldon Mercy Academy. This Vivaldi jam was really taking me back to my punk rock youth and I was playing it even louder than the 4 Non Blondes. Viper and I were headbanging in unison somehow again, Sammy looking shocked and annoyed that I could find a way to rock out to classical. The kids hopped out and I blew them kisses, then was on my way to Motorized Industries!

I got to my station and I saw my buddy Milo—his station being next to mine. "How was the weekend, Chico?" I told him how Viper scored five points in his basketball game Friday night and when we took him to the mall afterwards to celebrate and eat at California Pizza Kitchen, he was so happy and excited he kind of crapped in his pants on the way out and had dingleberries running down his leg. Then how on Saturday we saw that new, super-cheesy flick about young girls and horses cause Samantha wanted to see it, then spent all day Sunday at Phyllis' parents' house barbecuing, and how I mostly slept outside by their pool while everyone else played board games and drank Cokes.

"That's pretty fucking funny about the kid's shit coming down his leg, holmes! Fuck Papi! I needed that! My weekend *sucked*, man! You know, Papi, like with my people, man, mi familia, when you have a party, you know, you can't invite anybody but the family. My family is big, Papi, so, like, once you invite the family, it's like, *Boom!*, sixty people at least for sure are coming. Game over. So like, forget about meeting the ladies or whatever. It's like, put sixty pieces of corn and buy out Costco of all the hot dogs and burgers they got, put that shit on the grill and get ready to work, Papi."

"Woah! That sounds really intense, Milo!"

"It is Papi. Like, one year, for vacation, we had to rent an entire hotel outside of Las Vegas just for the family. Then we had no more money for anything else so for the whole trip we just sat by the pool (fig. 17)."

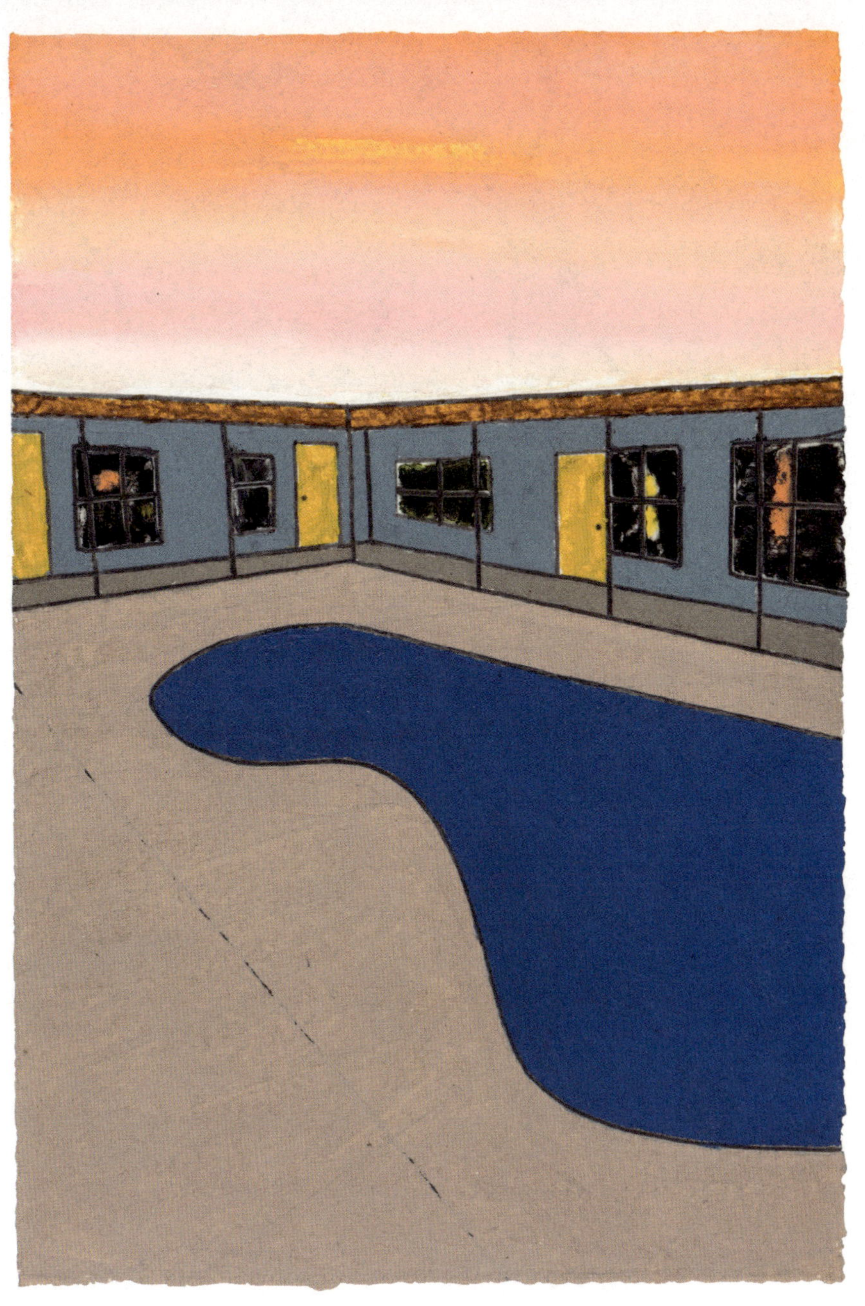

(fig. 17)

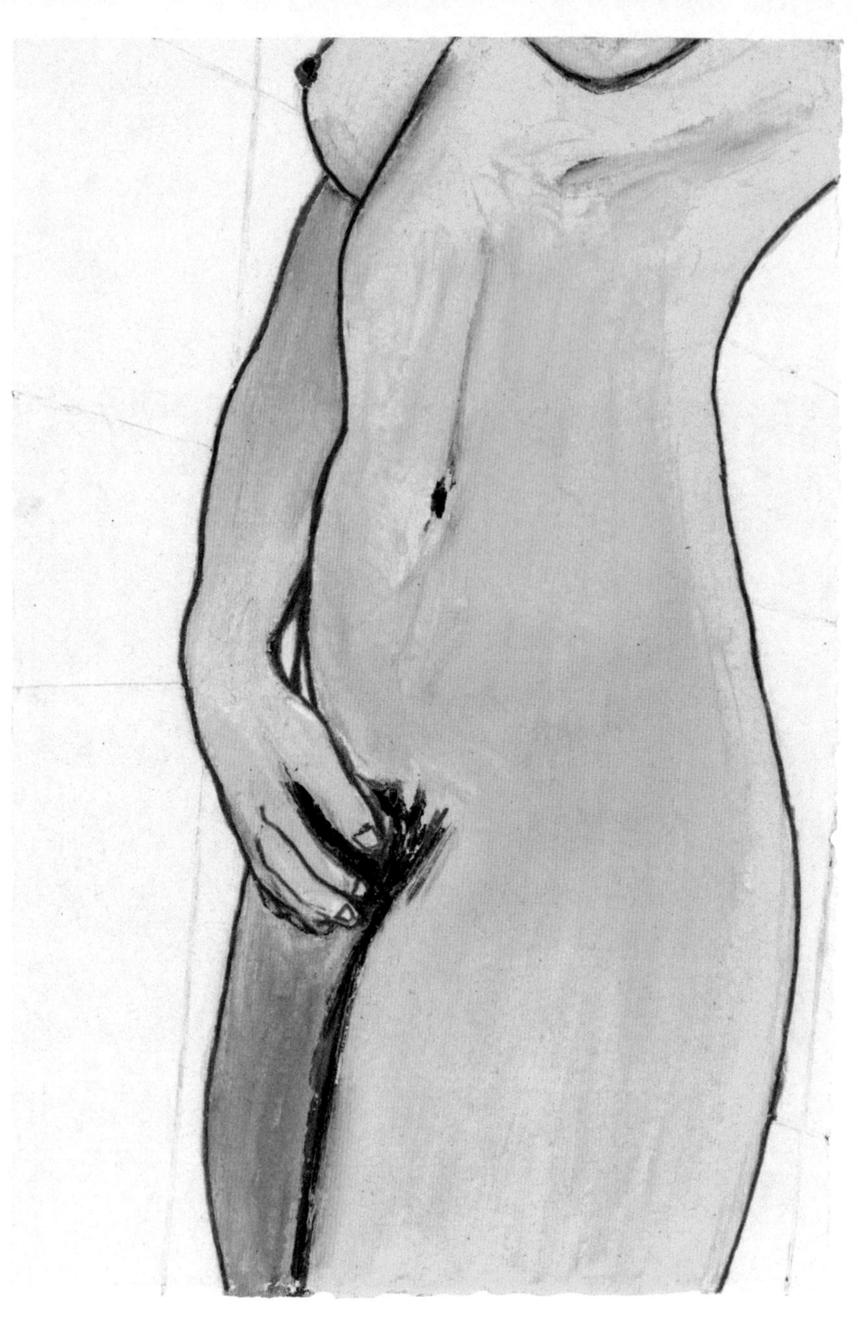

(fig. 18)

Derrick

I think I died in this little island-jumper plane I
was in with my girlfriend. We were on vacation
on our way to an island off of Costa Rica and
she must have survived the crash, or at least
she's not here with me now. Maybe I had a heart
attack. I don't remember what happened. But
all of a sudden I'm here. On this beach. The
temperature of the water is the same as the air. It
remains dusk, permanently. I see other people on
the beach but they are far away, and when I try
to walk towards them the distance remains the
same. I am never hungry or thirsty. I sleep often.
There is no way to gauge time. I doze off again.

I am dreaming about Dylan touching
herself in the shower (fig. 18) at our apartment
in LA and when I wake there is a man next
to me, fat and burnt-bacon tan. He's bald, but
what's left of his hair is past his shoulders, jet
black, and extremely greasy. He must be in his
fifties or sixties. He's got a gold chain with a
gold cross attached to it, gold boardshorts, and
chromed-out aviators hiding his eyes.

"Jesus. You startled me."

"Not Jesus. My name's Derrick."

"Where are we? Heaven?"

"We're in Puerto Rico, my friend."

"Puerto Rico is heaven?"

"Puerto Rico ain't heaven, but it's damn near close."

"I don't get it. I was on a plane with my girlfriend—" Derrick cut me off.

"Yeah. You didn't have a heart attack, if that's what you're thinking. The pilot and mechanic of your plane, Simon, he had a drinking problem. Forgot to check the oil and you all crashed. Nose-dived beautifully into the Pacific (fig. 19). Wish you could've seen it the way I did. You all died on impact and your bodies were eaten by sharks."

He stopped talking and pulled out a pack of smokes—Pall Mall Ibiza Sunsets, the ones where you squeeze the filter and the flavor goes crazy. The graphic on the carton looks like SkyBox basketball cards. These apparently were double-loaded—watermelon and cherry.

"Want a smoke?"

I was thinking about my girlfriend, Dylan.

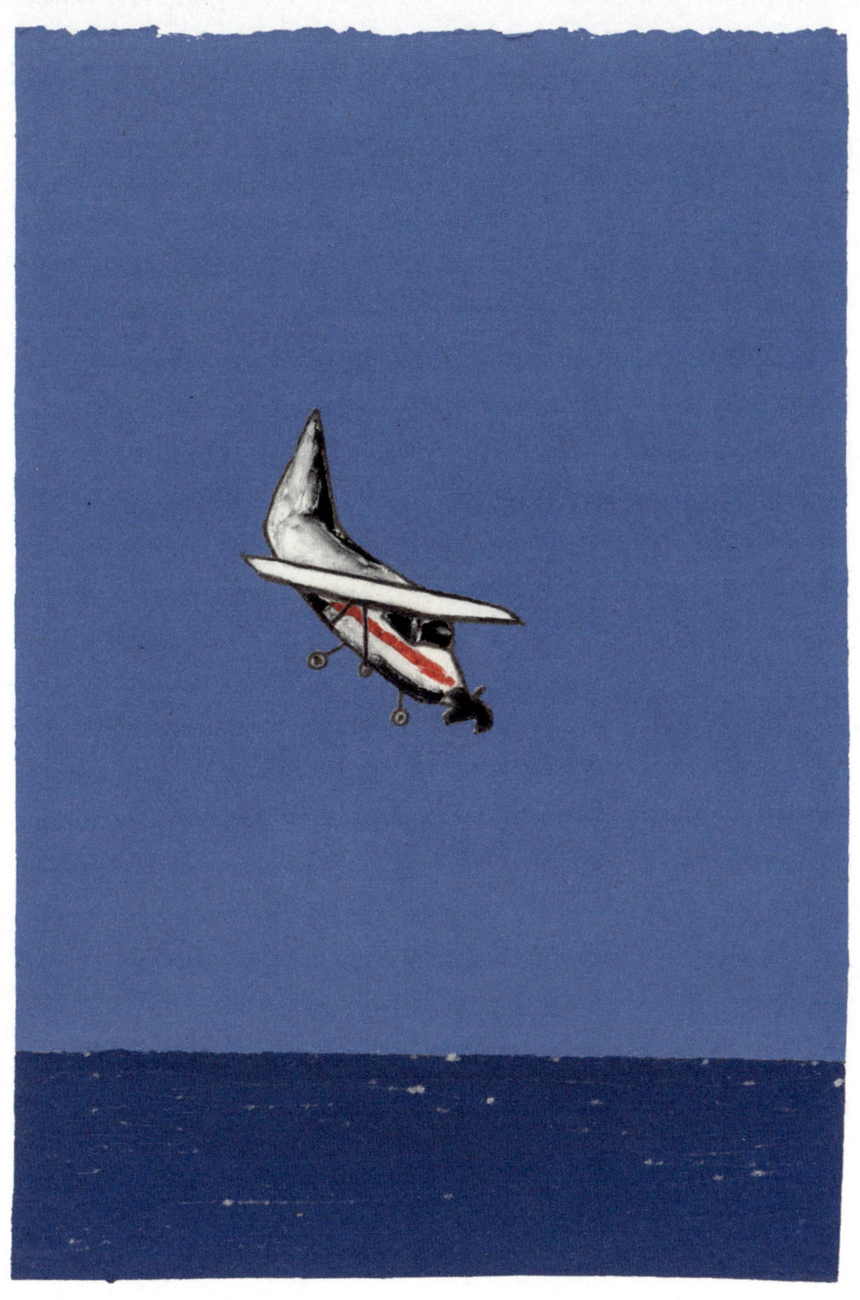

(fig. 19)

Where is she? Maybe on the beach or somewhere else in Puerto Rico? Strangely I wasn't sad or distraught at all. I was going to ask her to marry me.

"I said you want a smoke?"

"No thanks. I don't smoke."

"Dylan's fine. She's with my partner. Plus, have a smoke. You're dead man. It ain't gonna kill ya twice!"

"Your partner?"

"Yeah. She's with God. God hired me a while ago to run the business-side of things. God kinda got this whole shebang started and then needed help managing all sides of said business. All that stuff is pretty boring. Anyway, you're coming with me to a party tonight. I'll see you later."

He didn't suddenly vanish, or evaporate into thin air. He walked down to the edge of the water, cranked out fifty burpees on an incline, then somehow gracefully jumped into the ocean and swam until I couldn't see him anymore.

When I woke up the next time I was in full cowboy attire. Blue jeans, tan leather boots, red and green-checkered flannel shirt, and a really nice leather belt that had these two leather pouches attached to it. One had a knife and the other, surprisingly, an iPhone. I was standing, staring at the ocean, waiting for Derrick when I suddenly had both of my knees kicked in from the back.

"Gotcha! Hey Little Buddy, you're lookin' pretty sharp. Where'd you get that outfit?"

"I have no idea. I woke up with this on."

"Of course you did. Look Pete. Don't fuck with me, okay?"

"I'm not fucking with you Derrick. I have no idea—"

"I'm just fucking with you." Derrick still had nothing on except for his gold boardshorts, chrome aviators, and gold cross.

"I hope you like salsa. We're going dancing tonight. Ever been on the back of a hog before?"

"Is that what you're wearing?"

"You got a problem with it?" I quickly said no, remembering Derrick's relationship with God.

"Good. I wear these shorts everyday, man. Get used to it."

Suddenly I thought that this was it. This

is eternity. Me in a cowboy outfit hanging out with Derrick in Puerto Rico. Never eating. Never drinking. Not remembering dozing off all day. Never seeing the sun or the moon. But why did I have a knife and how did I have an iPhone?

"Man, you gotta get out of your head. So you ever been on the back of a Harley? Nuts to butts?"

"I have not."

"Well, get that cute li'l ass on and let's go."

Derrick had a massive motorcycle. He drove barefoot, still in those gold boardshorts. And when we rode I had to wrap my arms around his tanned, greasy belly.

The roads were horrible. Unpaved with huge holes everywhere. Dust, and holes, and rocks. Dust, and jungle covered in dust. It smelled like molasses. None of this deterred Derrick from full throttle ripping. I think he was aiming for the holes. I could barely hold on. He was so sweaty and oily I nearly fell off every thirty seconds.

What I did notice on this ride was that for the first time since I got to Puerto Rico, it was positively dark outside—the Harley's high beam illuminating a circle of roots, leaves, and branches covered in an ochre dust—and I thought I saw the moon. And somehow above the roar of Derrick's Harley, I heard the incessant drumbeat of cumbia. Dylan had wanted me to take salsa lessons with her, and, for the first time, I wish I had. As we got closer to the music, I could see that this was a full-on carnival. Loads of rides with flashing lights; I caught two huge dance halls and made out a rodeo ring.

Derrick yelled. "Pete, you gotta trust me this evening. Okay? With everything."

I yelled back. We kept yelling. "I mean, Derrick. Do I have a choice?"

"Hey. What did I tell you about fucking with me?"

"You're right. I was fucking with you!"

We parked in a field that was full of cows, 4×4s, and dirt bikes. Derrick's Harley literally looked like a chariot. He turned it off and there was a buzz.

"Loose'n up are we? Pete, take this and put it on." Derrick was holding a humongous, blue gardening hat.

"Really?"

"Man, I told you to trust me, right?"

"Yeah."

"So put it on."

I put it on. Derrick took my hand. We walked into the carnival, Derrick still wearing nothing but the gold boardshorts, his aviators, and gold Jesus-piece. Me in this cowboy outfit. Holding hands. I thought that I hadn't held hands with a man in public since I was a little kid holding my father's.

It was only local Puerto Ricans, families, and cowboys. Little, makeshift games everywhere. Like stacks of blocks where guys were heaving these heavy stones, trying to knock out the red block in the bottom-middle of a pyramid of them. Most of the games I couldn't understand what the objective was, but we played all of them. I tried balancing little green balls on top of smaller pink ones. I tried kicking a soccer ball into small bowling pins. There was that boxing one that tells you how hard your punch was. Another game where I was blindfolded, licking who knows what and trying to match tastes with different fruits.

And we went on all the rides. Derrick loved

the one where there's this big disc-like thing
and you sit down along the rim of the ride
and just hold on as it spins faster and faster.
Young boys standing in the middle of the disc,
dancing by tapping their feet with the rotations,
tapping faster and faster, trying to stay in the
same position. Getting taken down one by one
and smashing into the perimeter. People being
thrown out of their seats and onto the floor,
pinning everyone with a rapid centrifugal
force. We played bumper cars for a whole hour
straight. Derrick and I laughing our asses off
as we drilled little kids and their parents from
behind, whiplashing their necks. In the hall of
mirrors we scared the shit out of the same kids
when we would hop out at the end of a dead-end
corridor and scream in their faces. Somehow the
whole time in the hall of mirrors we never saw
our reflections.

"Pete, let's go drink for a little."

"There's a bar here?"

"Walk with me."

Derrick took my hand again. We walked
down the same alley of games and into a huge
dance hall—through an entranceway of silver,

shiny-streamers, like something marking the entrance to a high school dance.

"Pete, now this is Heaven."

"Really?"

"I mean, look around you. Look at all of these beautiful families and everybody dancing such beautiful salsa. Do you know how to dance?"

"Dylan wanted to take classes but, to be honest, I could never get into it and always made up excuses."

"Not tonight, my friend. C'mon. Let's hit the floor."

Derrick took my hand a third time and walked me onto the dance floor. He placed my right hand on his left hip and put his left hand on my right shoulder. Our other hands holding, high in the air. "Okay, Papi. Just follow me."

Despite how ridiculous we must have looked—Derrick barefoot in the gold boardshorts, sunglasses permanently on, topless and greasy, me in full on cowboy attire— nobody paid us any attention. And Derrick was an excellent dancer. With the same effortless and graceful manner as he'd done those burpees and swam into the sea, we glided on the dance floor together. He was staring me in the eyes; I could feel it.

"Don't look at your feet, Pete. Just trust me."

With cumbia, and Latin music in general, the music never stops. If you're in good shape and with the right partner you can dance forever. I looked up and Derrick's face was two inches away from mine, my blue hat like an umbrella over both of us. In his chrome aviators I saw only a silhouette of my face, the massive blue hat, and my flannel shirt. I couldn't tell if we danced for five minutes or five hours. He had no scent.

We were sitting down now on a few pieces of wood nailed together at a table made out of another few pieces of wood nailed together. Derrick even greasier and me covered in sweat. There were at least twelve empty beers on our table. We were just boozing right next to the speakers. And this too felt like a slip of time. No matter if we were drinking fast or drinking slow, I was feeling the local beers.

"Pete." I had somehow completely forgotten that Derrick was sitting right next to me.

"What are you thinking about?"

"Nothing. I mean, I'm just feeling really fucking good. I love this music. The lights are so cool."

Derrick looked serious. Still seated, dancing to the music in his chair, but staring at me straight-faced. He looked hammered. I couldn't see his eyes through the chrome, but I imagine them a little droopy, wasted. He was slouched over the table. I must have looked hammered too.

"What's up Derrick. Wanna go dance some more?"

"We're done with the dancing. You can dance great now. At least you can dance like a man. I'll teach you tomorrow night how to dance like a woman. Then you can find your own middle ground. But no more dancing. This next shit is serious. What time is it?"

"I have no idea."

"Check your phone."

As if normally, I went for the leather pouch with the iPhone in it. When I clicked the home button, the background was a close-up of Derrick's torso, showing his oily chest, lots of chest hair, his gold cross, and the top part of his gold boardshorts (fig. 20). I cracked up laughing.

"Hey. What's so funny?"

"Oh. Nothing. It's quarter to nine."

"Put that funny shit aside, Pete. Couple more beers at the bar and we're outta Heaven."

The place had thinned out. Just a few super drunk couples holding beers, still dancing. At the bar were seven cowboys and us. "You're one of them, Pete."

If looks are what Derrick was talking about, he was right. We were all more or less dressed the same. Different color flannels, but we all had great leatherwork—I noticed I had a big, screaming eagle belt buckle—blue jeans, nice boots with spurs and we were all wearing those huge gardening hats. A few of the cowboys had red ones.

"I look like one of them, Derrick. But I'm no cowboy. I've never even been on a horse."

"How 'bout you quit telling me what you are and what you aren't. We're at Heaven in fucking Puerto Rico, Pete. Do you understand? Do you get what is happening? What has happened?"

"Dude, yeah. I'm fucking dead. I died in that plane crash and now we hangout together.

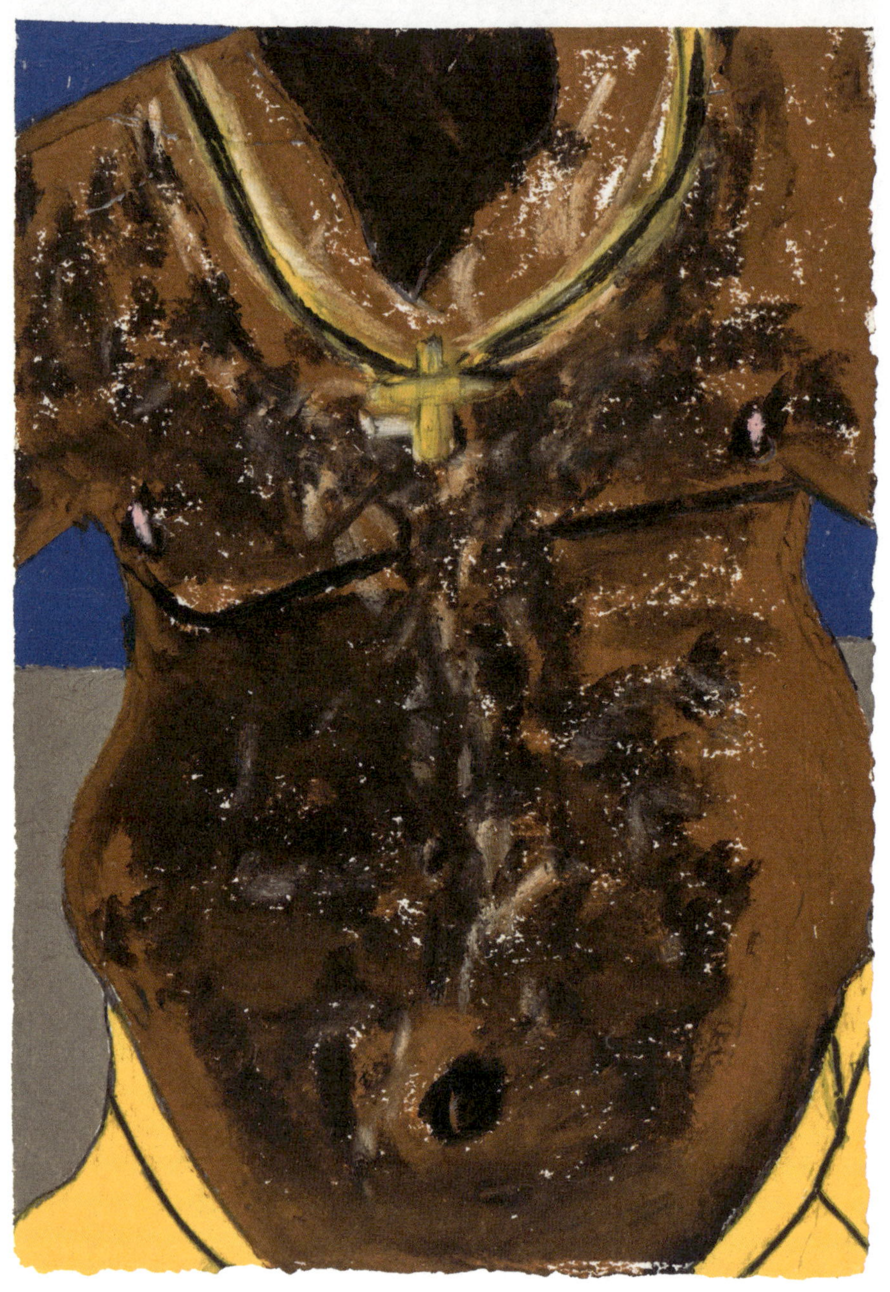

(fig. 20)

You're like God, but not God. I'm a cowboy. This is so much more fun than what I thought it was going to be. Like long, dirt nap. Fuck, Derrick. I'm so happy to meet you man."

Derrick just stared at me. More hammered-looking. He touched my knee and then he took me by the hand again and we stood up together, this time I think more to maintain his balance.

"We're going to the rodeo. You're on at nine."

I must have blacked out from the beers cause as soon as we walked out of Heaven, hand-in-hand through those silvery-shiny streamers, I don't remember anything. When I come to I am on top of an enormous, raging fucking bull. *Huuuuge* horns. In the cage-thing. My blue hat gone, replaced by what felt like a hockey helmet. My left hand is strapped irrevocably tight into the saddle with heavy rope that I'm gripping with a yellow leather glove. The rope strapping my palm, fingers plastered over the rope, three times done over. I'm holding onto the cage with my right hand and as some cowboy ties the rope tighter around the bull's balls it bucks in pain, cracking my entire skeletal system and sending my brain rattling around my skull. I catch eyes with the animal, briefly, through the bars in my helmet.

Then, all of a sudden, I am in the stands with Derrick, drinking beers. Looking at me on the bull. I turn to my left and look at Derrick leaning against the row behind us, smoking a Pall Mall and still wearing nothing but those gold boardshorts, gold Jesus-piece, and the chromed-out aviators. He turns and looks at me.

"This, my friend, is the best part."

A boy of about fifteen is in the ring, holding a rope attached to the cage's swing door, putting all of his weight against it. The door flies open. In bull riding, the deal is to make it to eight seconds. No score on anything less than eight. Then you are scored depending on your style and how nuts the bull is. My bull was absolutely fucking buck and I had mad style. My right arm doing these crazy helicopter swings, first on my right side, then over my head, and then in reverse all over again. The bull doing a full spin into a hard buck forward, followed by a spring-like jump on all four of its legs.

The buck forward sent my entire body over the bull's head. I saw my left arm crack under the pressure, but it kept me on. The bull then popped up on all fours and leaped, and my chin cracked hard against the top of the bull's head, knocking me unconscious. The bell signaled eight seconds and the crowd went nuts. Derrick cracked me on the back. "Look at you go! Now watch this."

The crowd's cheers turned to a collective gasp when they noticed that I was knocked out and dangling on the bull's right side, attached only by the left hand secured to my saddle. With the bull running along the perimeter of the ring, a circular gasp ricocheted around the rodeo.

"Pete. Are you ready?"

"What the fuck, Derrick? Ready for what?"

"Watch!"

I was still in the stands sitting next to Derrick, but I was seeing and feeling what I was feeling and seeing as if I were the me on the bull. I regained consciousness. All I see is black hide, hooves, and dirt all blurred together. I realize I am hanging off the side of the bull, going incredibly fast. With my free right hand, bloodied from being dragged on the ground, I reach for the smaller leather pouch—the one with the knife inside. Derrick gave me a switchblade. I could feel the button. I pressed it and, with my left arm still attached, pulled myself up enough to cut the rope that held it locked in place. Once free, I draped off the animal.

Now my vision and feeling switched back. I was next to Derrick, watching. He was leaning forward, hands on his knees, mouth agape. I looked back to the ring when I heard another collective gasp. I had fallen off and the bull was pummeling me, ignoring all the clowns and cowboys who were trying to get it away. One of them took an electric prodder and cracked it in its ass. As it turned to rear around from the shock, its back left hoof cracked hard on my helmet, shattering the plastic and my skull. Bouncing into and off of the dirt. A thud. Screams. Black.

I woke up this time.

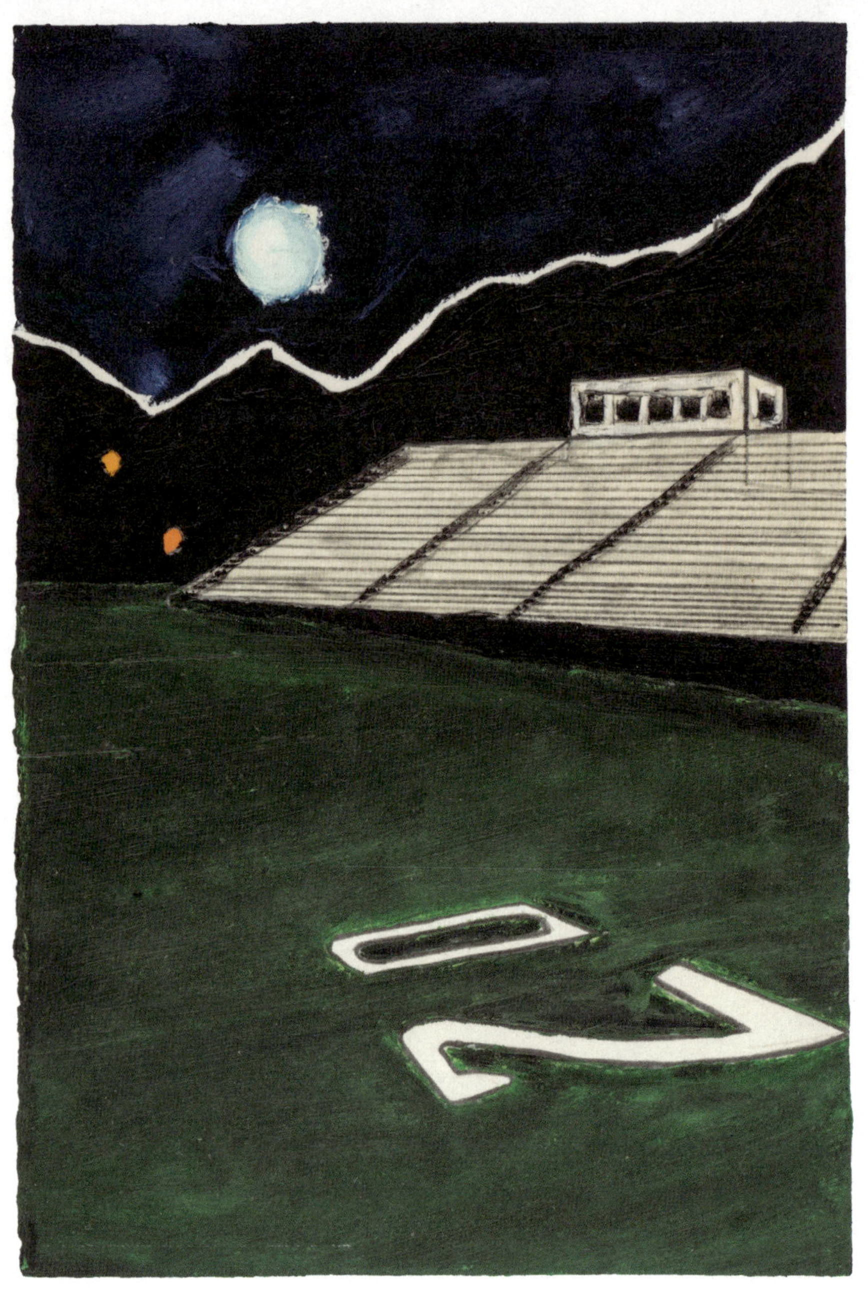

(fig. 21)

Hello!

Jamie Silverdreme and Chris Leftway are fourteen and fifteen years old. The date is February, the third or fourth. We find these boys on their backs next to one another in the middle of Sticksville High's football field (fig. 21), looking up into the wintery, starry night. The stadium lights are off. Behind them, a low frequency vibration from power lines gives the air a buzz.

Their science teacher, Mr. McElroy, has been teaching them about distance and light. How light travels faster than sound. Or maybe how sound travels faster than light. And then, two days ago, Mr. McElroy got the flu and the substitute teacher, Ms. Iverson, was put in charge. They would sit across from each other and raise their hands so that Ms. Iverson would come behind, let's say Jamie, so that, let's say Chris, could peer inside Ms. Iverson's blouse while she leaned over Jamie's textbook to tell him something about one age being before another age.

The learning process turns out to be, indeed, curved. But there wasn't going to be any of that during this lesson. "Boys and girls, Mr. McElroy won't be in for the next week. He's got a pretty bad case of the flu. But he told me what you have been studying and I'd like you all to take this note home, have your parents read it, and bring it back to me." The proposal read as such:

Dear Parents,
Mr. McElroy has come down with a pretty bad case of the flu and he won't be in for the next week. I understand he's been teaching your children about distance and light. Before proceeding with this line of inquiry, I suggest that your children and I begin watching the entire *Back to the Future* series, some of the best films to encapsulate these concepts. Please check the box under either "Agree" or "Disagree." If you disagree, your children will simply have two periods of Phys. Ed. with Mr. Pourweiser.
[   ] Agree   [   ] Disagree
Sally Iverson
Sticksville Middle/High School

Jamie's and Chris' parents both checked the agree box. So for the next week in school, Jamie and Chris and all of their other classmates—with the exception of the O'Connor twins whose parents protested that the film didn't align with their religious viewpoints—had one of the best cinematic experiences of their youth. After cramming them all in by Friday, Ms. Iverson said that she wanted all of the students to pair up over the weekend, think about what they learned with Mr. McElroy, combine it with what they learned from the *Back to the Future*, and to not only come up with a wild idea like Doc, but also to try it out in the form of a science project.

For Jaime and Chris, that week of school was the best of their lives. For once it seemed like learning didn't consist of the normal stuff. Like memorize this chemical chart, prove these algorithms, learn what parts of the world go where and what their capitals are. This project wasn't about dividing and conquering. It was fun.

"Chris."

"Yeah."

"I was thinking about that project Ms. Iverson gave us."

"Me too."

"What if we borrowed one of those spotlight things your dad rents to school for the football games and we use it like a projector?"

"What do you mean?"

"Like we could mask out some words to tell our future selves. Blast it into the future."

"That sounds cool!"

"Yeah. Like, *Hello!*" Jaime shouted the word past the twenty yard line. They both started shouting *Hello!* down field.

"I'll ask my dad tonight at dinner. We've been talking a lot about *Back to the Future*. He told me he saw all of them in the theaters."

"That's so cool."

Chris and Jamie spent the next forty-five minutes looking up at the sky. Not talking. Chris saw a shooting star—*Wouah!*—that Jamie missed.

They saw the moon rise up over their houses while walking home. Jamie split from Chris at Mill and Greenblatt. Chris went up one more street on Mill, to Feather. He could see Jamie's window at night. Chris could see his.

"See you tomorrow!"

"Yeah! But call me later. Let me know what your dad says."

"Cool."

...

"Hi Mrs. Silverdreme. It's Chris Leftway. May I please speak with Jamie?"

"Hi Chris. Of course you can. One second, sweetie. *Jaaaaaaammmmmieeeeeee. Chris is on the phone for you.*' Thanks Mom! I'll take it up here!"

"Chris?"

"Jamie."

"Thanks Mom. I got it. 'Goodnight Chris.'"

"Goodnight Mrs. Silverdreme."

"So, what happened?"

"It was crazy. When I came home Dad was doing barbecue and Nicole and Mom were inside. I could smell Dad's ribs as soon as I turned onto Feather."

"So lucky. We had veggie casserole. But what about the project?"

"Yeah. So when I smelled that and saw my sis and Mom inside, I was like, I'm gonna walk right outside and ask Dad."

"Yeah, and?"

"So I said, 'Dad. It smells so good. I smelled it around the corner!'"

"Chris!"

"Dude, I asked him and he said yes! Thought it was a super cool idea and he has one available."

"What?!"

"Yeah!"

"Your dad is so cool."

"Yeah. So what do you think?"

"About what?"

"What's our message to us?"

"What do you think?"

"I like the *Hello!* (fig. 22)" Chris trailed off on a long *O*.

"Let's do it!"

"Okay, cool. I'll get some tape and cardboard and see you on the field tomorrow at nine."

"Cool! Goodnight Chris."

"Night Jamie."

Now, Chris and Jamie didn't get to witness this part. After the dance that spring, they'd forgotten all about the experiment. In fact, nobody thought about it for a very long time. A *very* long time. In this instance, we're talking twenty-five-trillion light years. That's 1.47 times

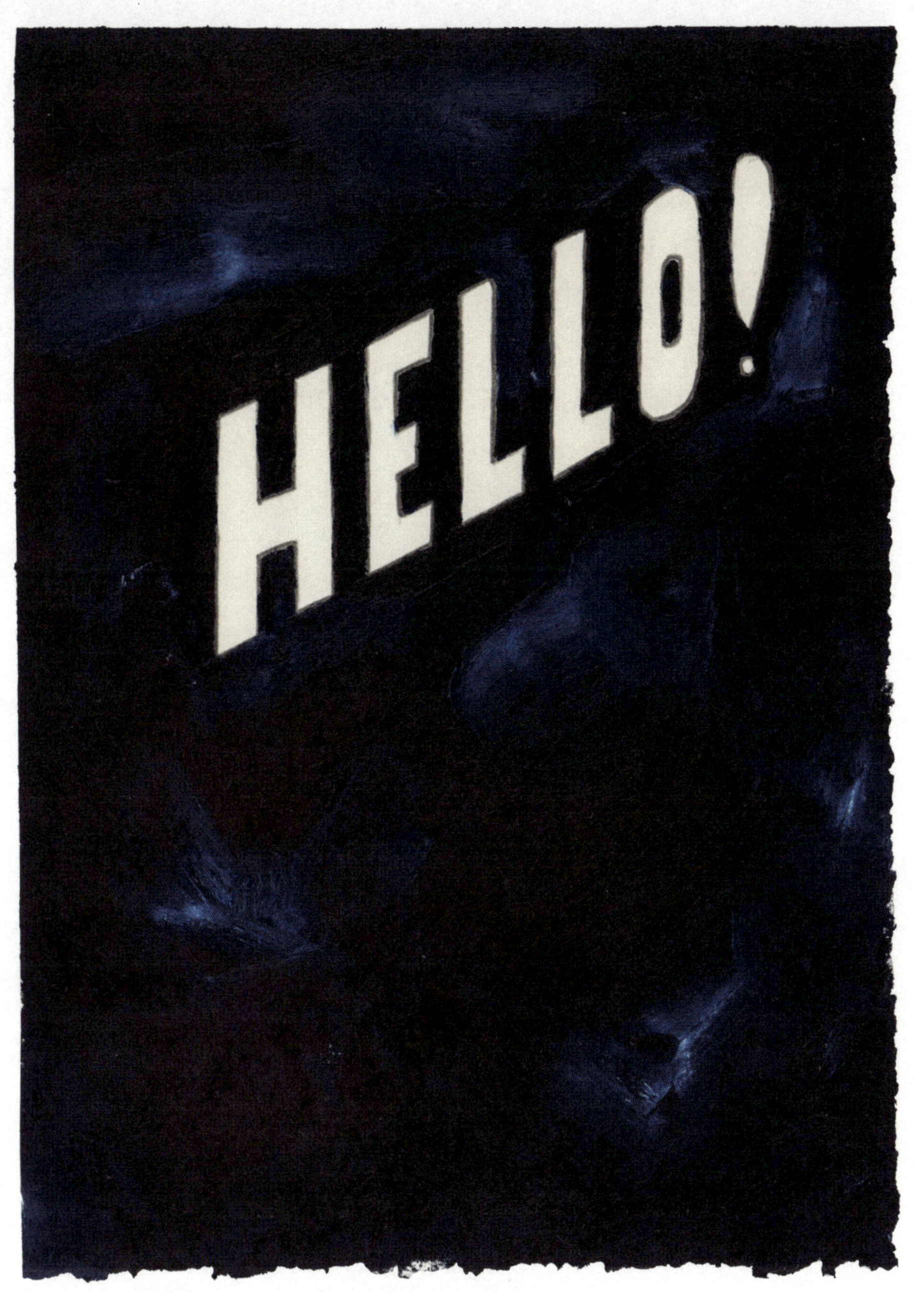

(fig. 22)

10 to the 26th power miles. This distance. This time. Try doing the math on that. It's a long ways away. But it got there. Joey and Vinny were sitting on Vinny's stairs when they both saw a flash of light that said *Hello!*

"Bro. I'm tripping."

"Wha?"

"Swear ta God, I just saw some shit."

"Wha?"

"Like some flash or some shit."

"Wha?"

"Yeah. Like *Hello!*"

Vinny stretched the *O* for as long as he could. They were smoking Newports. Vinny was inhaling when he saw the *Hello!* and started talking. So he was all inhaling and talking at the same time, kind of like when you're about to burp in the middle of a sentence, and on the *O* he was exhaling.

"Dude. I feel a little weeuhd sayin' this. But I saw the same Goddamn thing."

"Bro."

"I'm sendin' this back."

"😜" (fig. 23)

"Genius!"

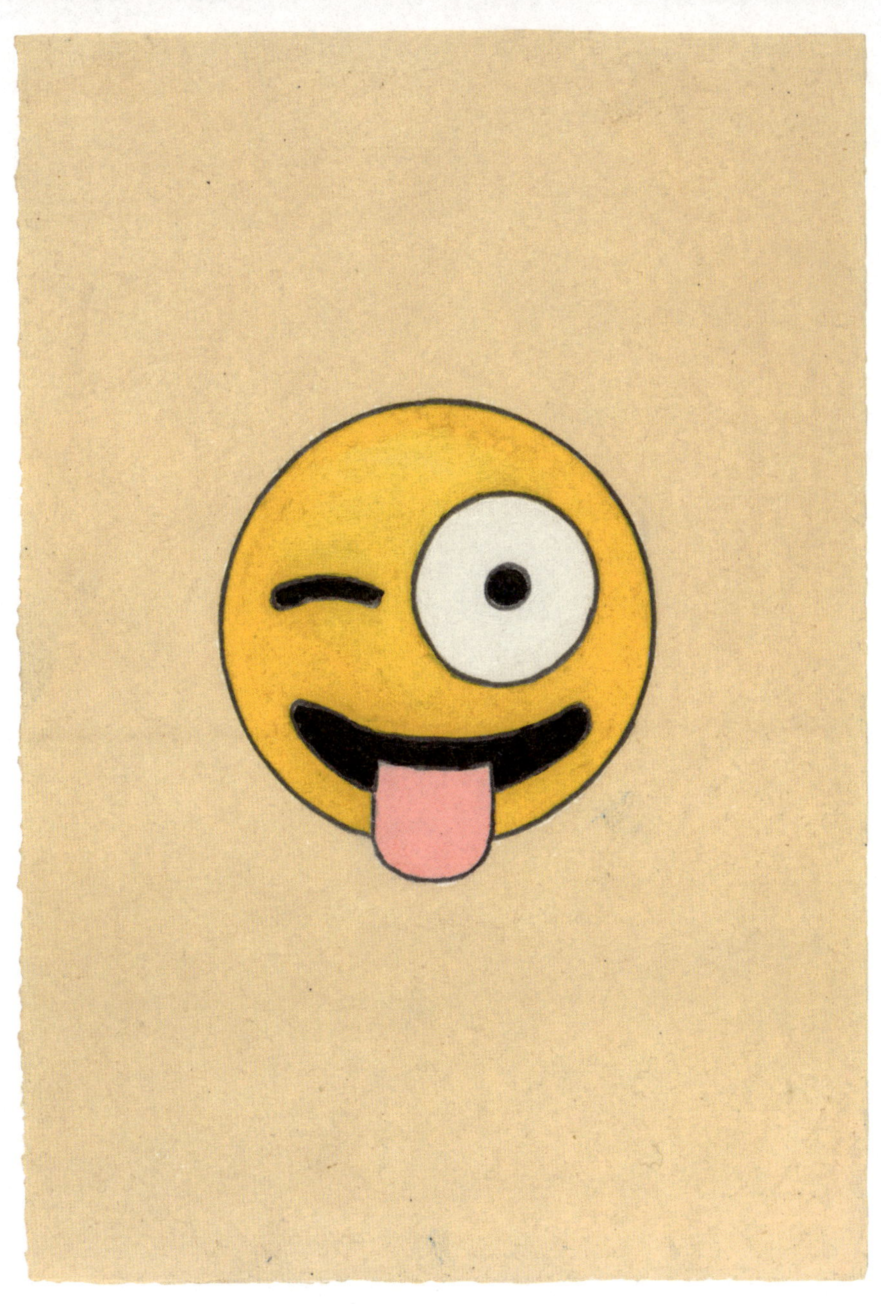

(fig. 23)

The End

Index of Works

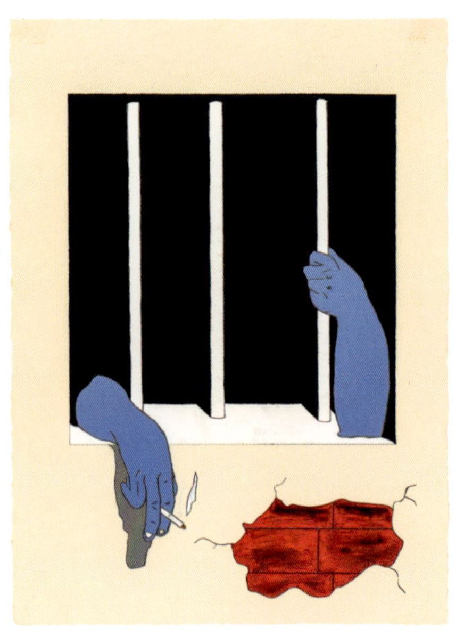

(fig. 0)

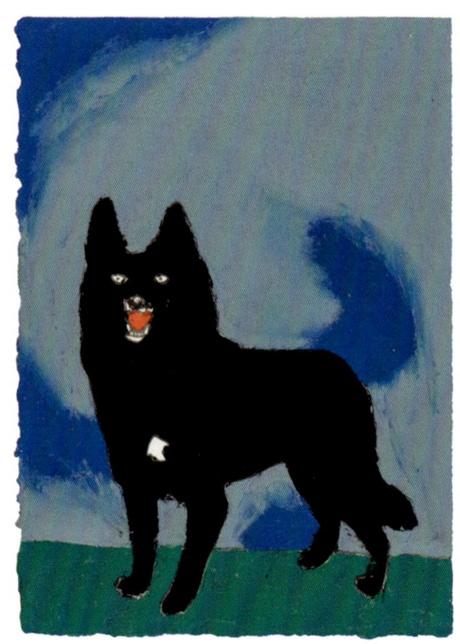

(fig. 1)

Peter in Prison
2019
77 × 58 cm
Oil stick and
pencil on paper

Buddy
2019
21 × 16 cm
Oil stick and
pencil on paper

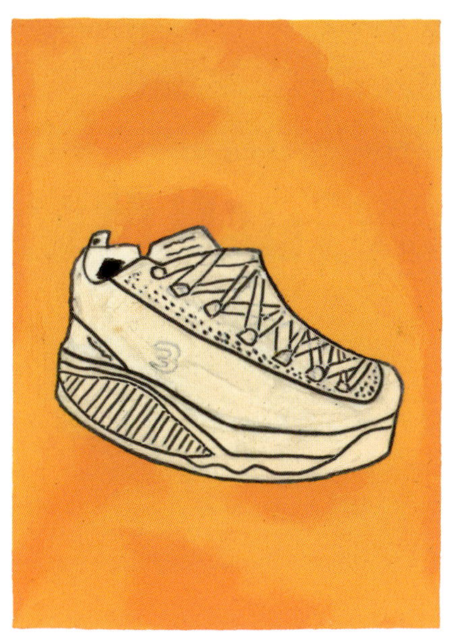

(fig. 2)

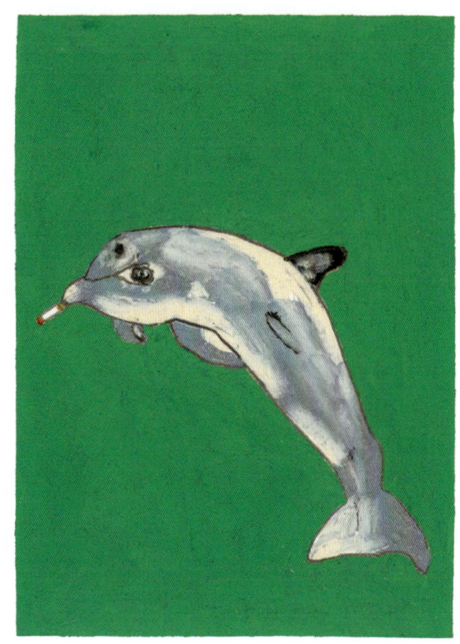

(fig. 3)

Pete's Shoes
2019
21 × 16 cm
Oil stick and
pencil on paper

Pete's Tie
2019
21 × 16 cm
Oil stick and
pencil on paper

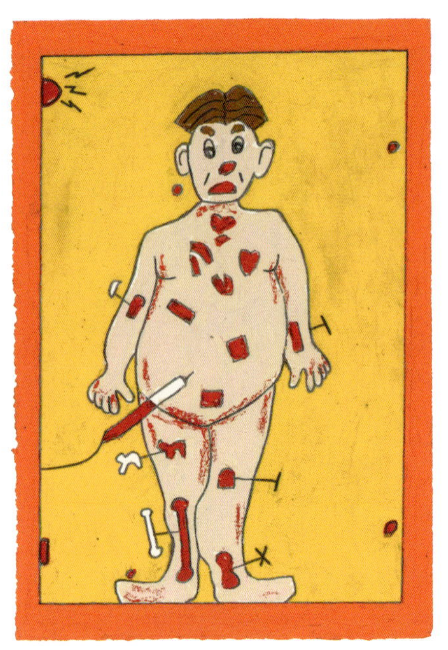

(fig. 4)

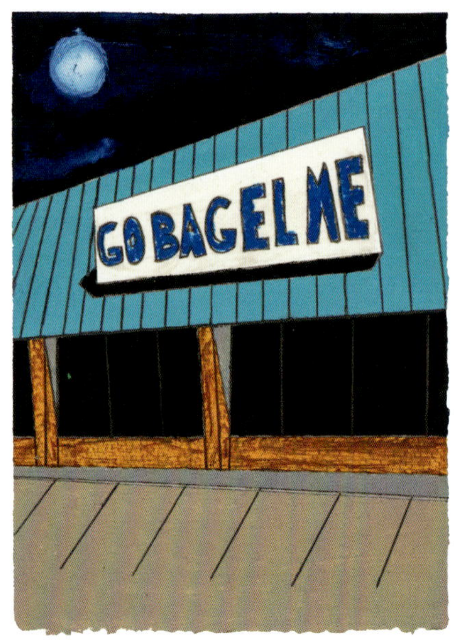

(fig. 5)

Operation
2019
30 × 21 cm
Oil stick and
pencil on paper

Go Bagel Me
2019
28 × 21 cm
Oil stick and
pencil on paper

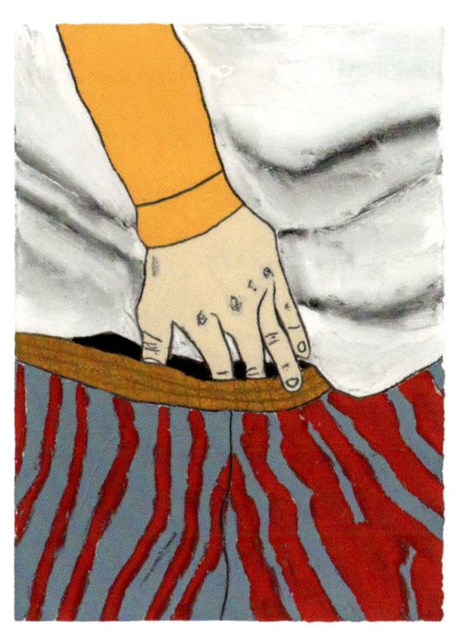

(fig. 6)

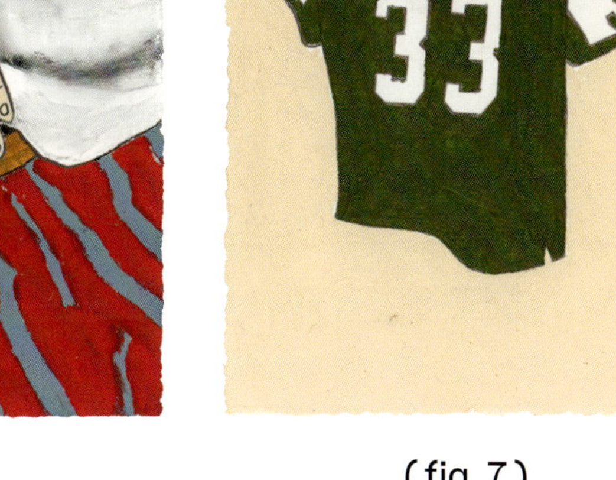

(fig. 7)

Jane
2019
28 × 21 cm
Oil stick and
pencil on paper

Riddles
2019
29 × 21 cm
Oil stick and
pencil on paper

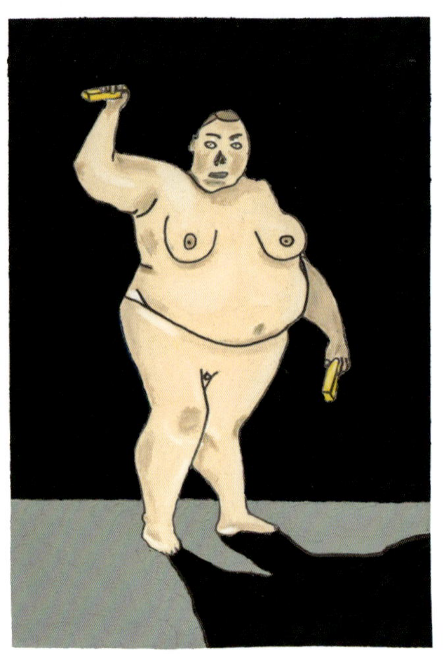

(fig. 8)

Psychoslut
  2019
  30 × 21 cm
  Oil stick and
  pencil on paper

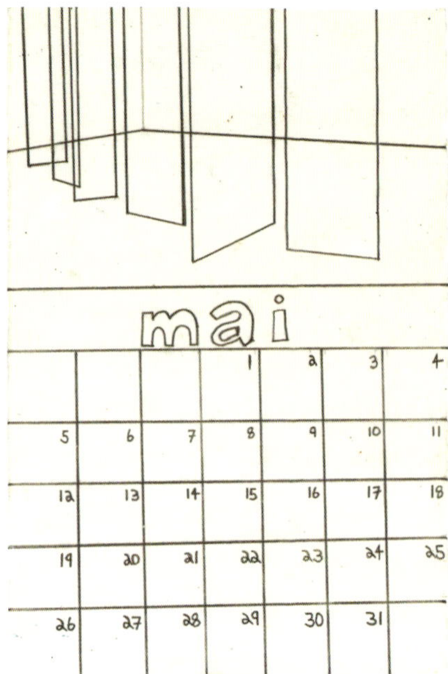

(fig. 9)

Cindy
  2019
  30 × 21 cm
  Oil stick and
  pencil on paper

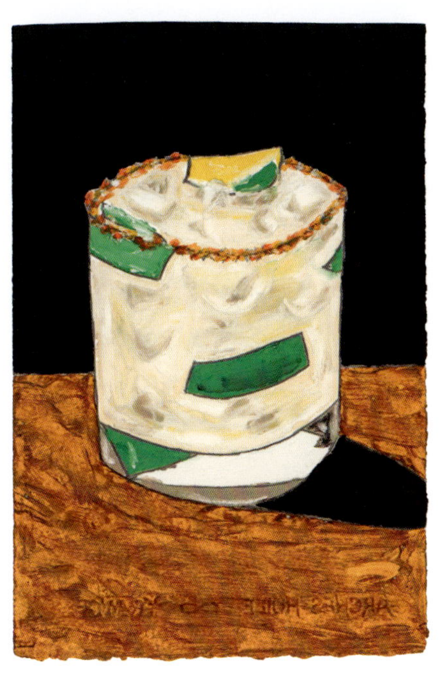

(fig. 10)

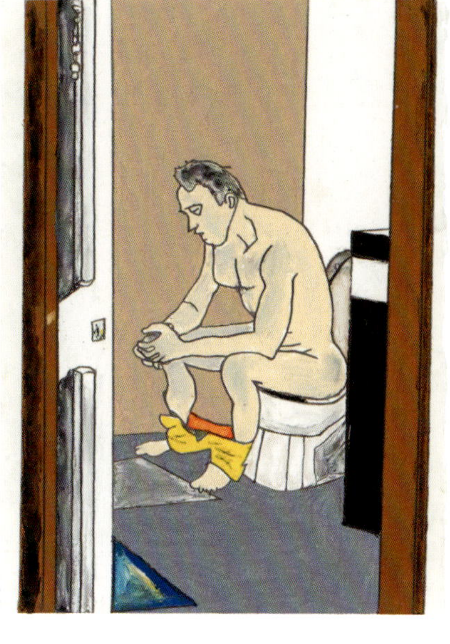

(fig. 11)

Mezcal Margarita
2019
30 × 21 cm
Oil stick and
pencil on paper

Good Morning
2019
31 × 24 cm
Oil stick and
pencil on paper

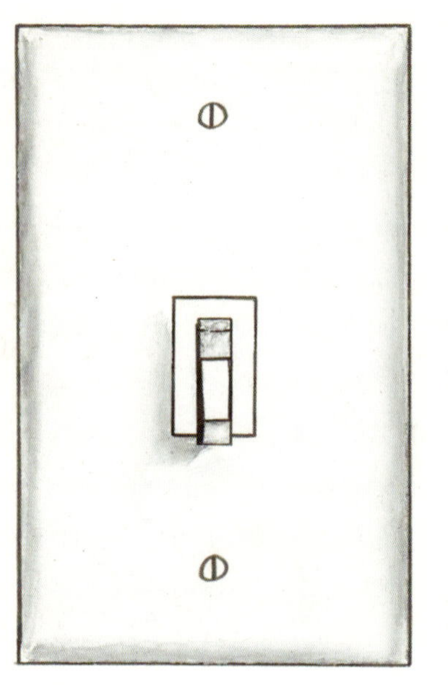

(fig. 12)

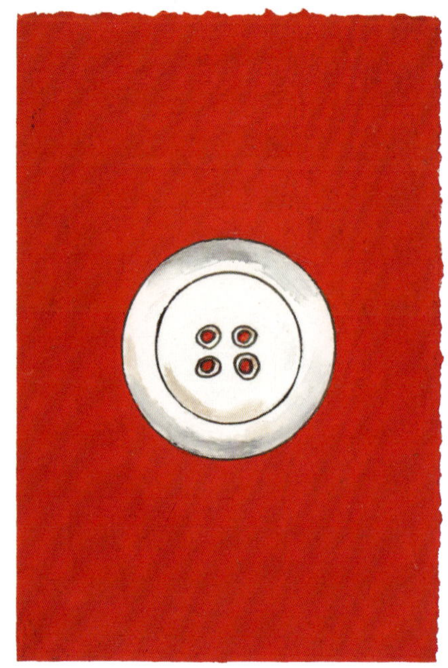

(fig. 13)

Light Switch
  2019
  24 × 16 cm
  Oil stick and
  pencil on paper

Button
  2019
  24 × 16 cm
  Oil stick and
  pencil on paper

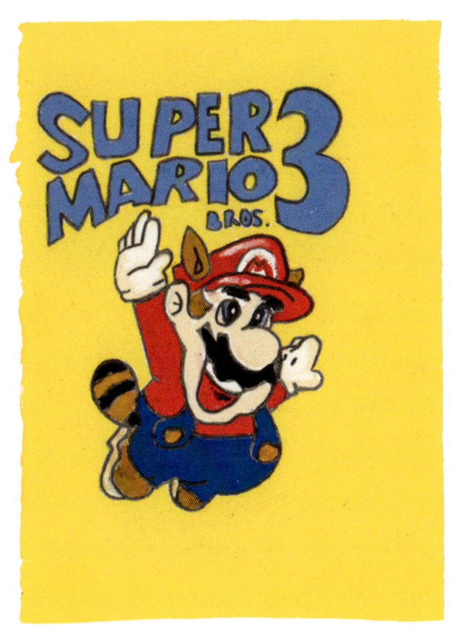

(fig. 14)

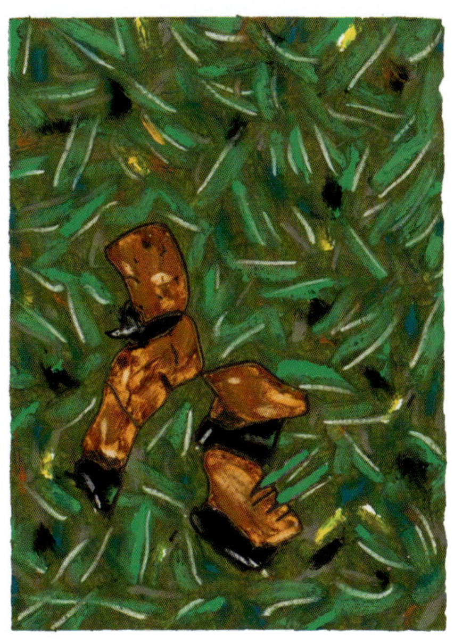

(fig. 15)

Super Mario Bros. 3
2019
21 × 16 cm
Oil stick and
pencil on paper

Dingy's Poop
2019
21 × 16 cm
Oil stick and
pencil on paper

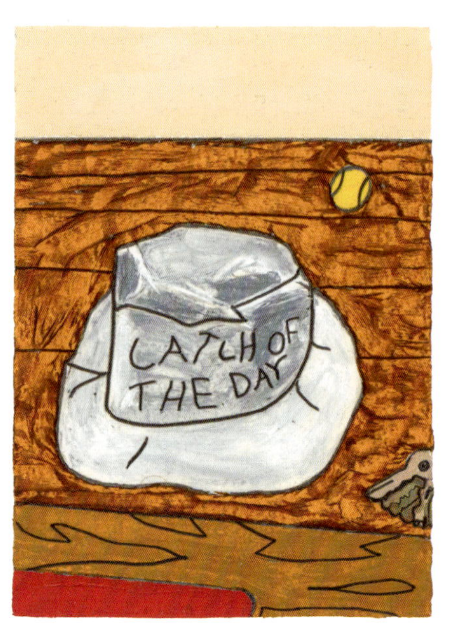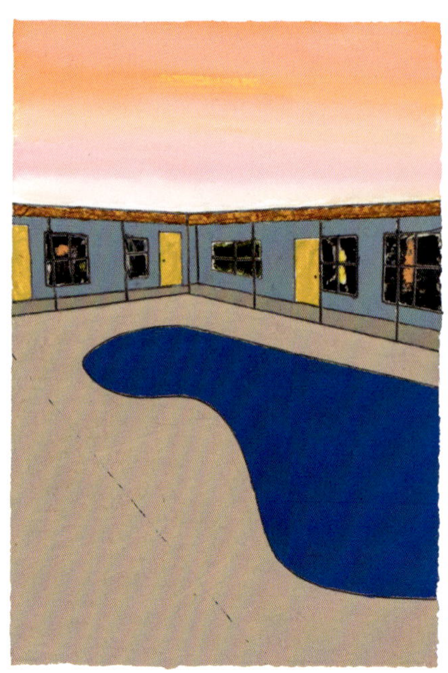

(fig. 16)   (fig. 17)

Viper's Hat
   2019
   21 × 16 cm
   Oil stick and
   pencil on paper

The Pool
   2019
   30 × 21 cm
   Oil stick and
   pencil on paper

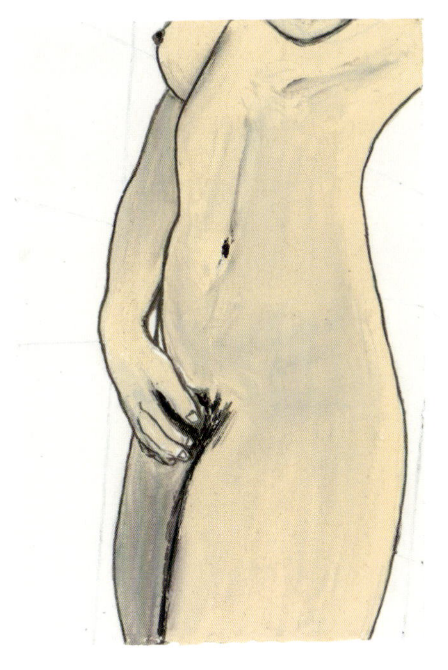

(fig. 18)

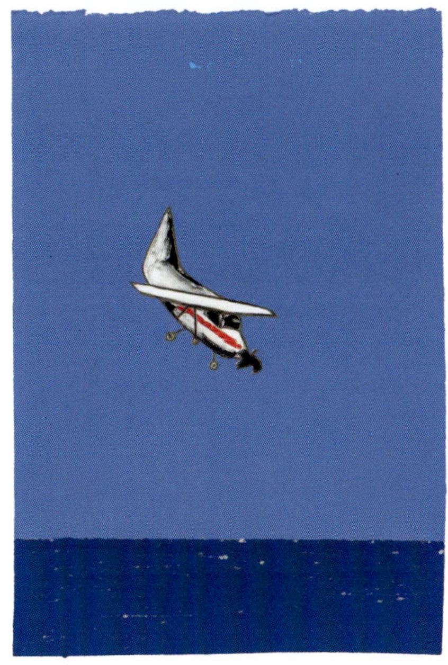

(fig. 19)

Dylan
2019
30 × 21 cm
Oil stick and
pencil on paper

Nose Diving
2019
30 × 21 cm
Oil stick and
pencil on paper

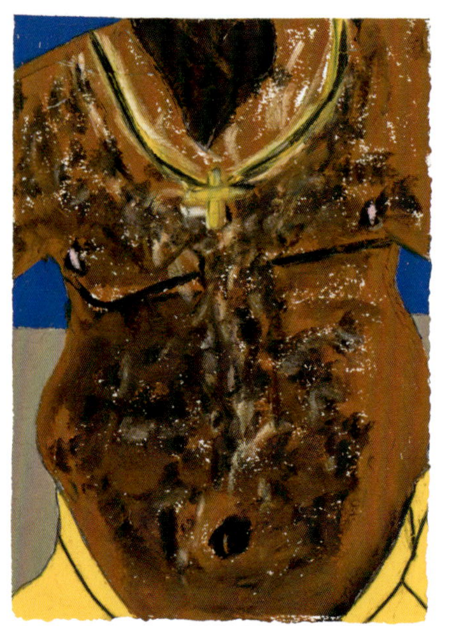

(fig. 20)

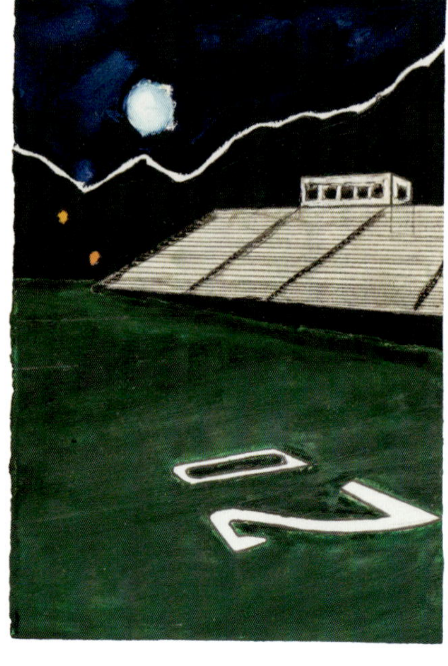

(fig. 21)

Derrick
  2019
  29 × 21 cm
  Oil stick and
  pencil on paper

Sticksville High
Football Stadium
  2019
  30 × 21 cm
  Oil stick and
  pencil on paper

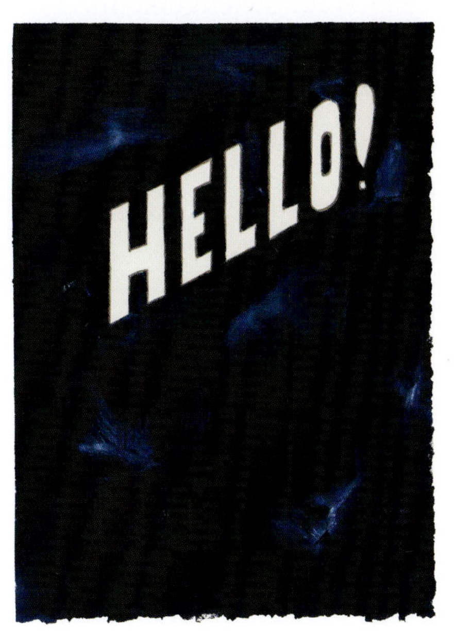

(fig. 22)

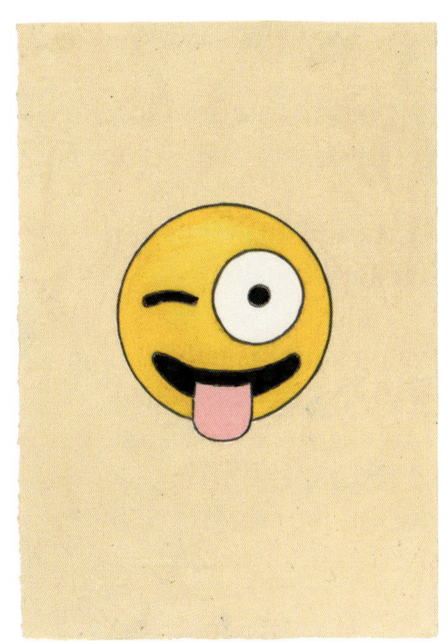

(fig. 23)

Hello!
2019
28 × 21 cm
Oil stick and
pencil on paper

;-)
2019
29 × 21 cm
Oil stick and
pencil on paper

Publisher Notes

Sticksville was produced in
a limited run of 400 copies.

Texts and drawings are
by Marc Breslin.

Alongside this publication,
a silkscreen heightened
with oil stick was produced
at 100 copies. All copies
are unique and signed by
the artist.

All rights reserved. No parts
of this publication may be
reproduced or transmitted,
in any form or by any
other means, without prior
permission of the publisher.

First edition (c) 2019
ISBN 978-84-09-12940-9

www.zolo.press

Acknowledgements

Marc Breslin thanks:

my Mother and Father,
David and John Breslin,
Lita Albuquerque,
Harold Ancart, Olivier Babin,
Bacon, Arno Baudin,
Angela Baudin García,
Bemelmans, Emily Blanchard,
Charlotte vander Borght,
Madeleine Braun,
Andrea Bustillos,
George Colimitra,
Jake Coulter, Brendan Dugan,
Tony Eble, Bill Fiore,
Uncle Frank, Cathy Gilroy,
Jenny Holzer, Karen Huber,
Adam Kleinman,
David Kordansky, Abby Leigh,
Robert Levine, Loosies,
Brian Lotti, Hector Madera,
Al Page, Valerie Passano,
Joe's Pizza, Pokey,
Alisa Post, Tom Powers,
Loup Sarion, Cindy Schwartz,
Nick Serpentine,
Robyn Siegel,
Benjamin Trigano,
Robbie C. Williamson,
Danh Võ.

Colophon

Publisher	Zolo Press
Editors	Marc Breslin
	Arno Baudin
Design	Arno Baudin
Editorial Assistant	Angela Baudin García
Copyediting & Proofreading	Robert Levine
Production	Marc Panero
Color Separation	Olivier Dengis
Printer	Agpograf, Barcelona
Paper	Munken print white
	Fedrigoni freelife gloss
	Colorplan bright white
Typography	GT Alpina by Grillitype
	Phase by Elias Hanzer